Qualitative Methods in Economics

Despite numerous books on research methodology, many have failed to present a complete, hands-on, practical book to lead college classes or individuals through the research process. We are seeing more and more scientific papers from all research fields that fail to meet the basic criteria in terms of research methods, as well as the structure, writing style and presentation of results. This book aims to address this gap in the market by providing an authoritative, easy to follow guide to research methods and how to apply them.

Qualitative Methods in Economics is focused not only on the research methods/techniques but also the methodology. The main objective of this book is to discuss qualitative methods and their use in economics and social science research. Chapters identify several of the research approaches commonly used in social studies, from the importance of the role of science through to the techniques of data collection. Using an example research paper to examine the methods used to present the research, the second half of this book breaks down how to present and format your results successfully.

This book will be of use to students and researchers who want to improve their existing research methods and read up on new and cutting edge methodological developments, as well as those who want to study ways to improve the research process.

Mirjana Radović-Marković is a full professor of Entrepreneurship at Akamai University, Hilo, Hawaii.

Beatrice Avolio Alecchi is a full professor of Accounting at CENTRUM Católica Graduate Business School, Lima, Peru.

Routledge Frontiers of Political Economy

Qualitative Methods in Economics

**Mirjana Radović-Marković
and Beatrice Avolio Alecchi**

LONDON AND NEW YORK

First published 2017 by Routledge

2 Park Square, Milton Park, Abingdon, Oxfordshire OX14 4RN
52 Vanderbilt Avenue, New York, NY 10017

Routledge is an imprint of the Taylor & Francis Group, an informa business

First issued in paperback 2019

British Library Cataloguing in Publication Data
A catalogue record for this book is available from the British Library

Library of Congress Cataloging in Publication Data
Names: Marković, Mirjana Radović, author. | Alecchi, Beatrice E. Avolio,
author.
Title: Qualitative methods in economics / Mirjana Radović-Marković and
Beatrice Avolio Alecchi.
Description: Abingdon, Oxon ; New York, NY : Routledge, 2017.
Identifiers: LCCN 2016014938| ISBN 9781138692473 (hardback) |
ISBN 9781315532257 (ebook)
Subjects: LCSH: Economics—Methodology. | Qualitative research.
Classification: LCC HB131 .M37 2017 | DDC 330.072/1—dc23
LC record available at https://lccn.loc.gov/2016014938

ISBN: 978-1-138-69247-3 (hbk)
ISBN: 978-0-367-88954-8 (pbk)

Typeset in Times New Roman
by Book Now Ltd, London

To my family, my life's great treasure. They are my source of inspiration for everything I undertake in life.

Beatrice Avolio Alecchi

I would like to thank my family for their unconditional love and support always.

Mirjana Radović-Marković

Contents

Illustrations

Figures

Tables

Boxes

About the authors

Mirjana Radović-Marković

Academician Radović-Marković is a full professor of Entrepreneurship. She holds a BSc, MSc and PhD degrees in Economics, as well as conducting research in Post-Doctoral Studies in Multidisciplinary Studies. After completing her dissertation, she continued her advanced studies in the Netherlands, the USA and Russia.

Her scientific career began at the Economics Institute in Belgrade and continued later at the Institute of Economic Sciences, also in Belgrade. Meanwhile, she was engaged full-time and part-time as a professor in numerous universities worldwide. She teaches 'Entrepreneurship' at the University of Kragujevac (Serbia) and at the Faculty of Business and Entrepreneurship in Belgrade (Serbia), as well as teaching 'Applied Business Economics and Entrepreneurship' at the Irish University Business School, London; 'Female Entrepreneurship' at Akamai University, Hilo, Hawaii; 'Principles of Entrepreneurship – Applications for Genealogy Business' at the American School of Genealogy, Heraldry & Documentary Sciences, Como, Mississippi; and 'Entrepreneurship and Female Entrepreneurship' at the International College of Management and Technology (ICMT) – Center for Women and Gender Studies, Nigeria. In addition, she has taught worldwide classes on subjects such as 'Women as Entrepreneurs' and 'Global Challenge' as part of the Global Virtual Faculty (GVF) Program at Fairleigh Dickinson University, New Jersey.

Since 2004 to the current day, Prof. Dr Mirjana Radović-Marković has been employed full time at the Institute of Economic Sciences in Belgrade. She is Chairman of the Scientific Board, Head of the Center for Economic Researches and a member of the Managing Board of the Institute of Economic Sciences. Since 2012 she has also been employed as a full professor at the Faculty of Business Economics and Entrepreneurship, Belgrade, and as a professor at the Belgrade Banking Academy – Faculty of Finance, Monetary Economy and Insurance (PhD program).

In addition, she is Editor-in-Chief of the journals *Economic Analysis* and *Journal of Women's Entrepreneurship and Education* and a member of the editorial board of five international peer-review journals, one of which is on the Thomson Reuters list.

By invitation, she has given a number of lectures abroad. She gave a presentation during the meeting of OECD experts in Istanbul in March 2010 and has delivered lectures at numerous colleges and universities, including: the Said Business School, University of Oxford (2010); Franklin College, Lugano, Switzerland (2011); the Faculty of Economics, University of Miskolc, Hungary (2009); the University St Kliment Ohridski, Sofia, Bulgaria (2012, 2013, 2014 and 2015); the University of Wroclaw, Poland (2014); and the Academy of Sciences and Arts of the Republic of Srpska, Banja Luka, Bosnia and Herzegovina (2014).

She is a Fellow of Academia Europaea, Fellow of the Royal Society of the Arts in the United Kingdom, and Fellow of the World Academy of Art and Science. In addition, she is also academician of EMAAS, Greece; elected fellow (full fellowship) of the European Academy of Sciences and Arts, Salzburg, Austria; elected secretary of Academia Europaea, Serbian Chapter; elected academician (full fellowship) of the Bulgarian Academy of Sciences and Arts, Sofia, Bulgaria; and academician and vice president of the Serbian Royal Academy of Scientists and Artists.

Radović-Marković has written 32 books and more than 200 peer-reviewed articles.

Beatrice Avolio Alecchi

Dr Beatrice Avolio Alecchi holds a PhD in Strategic Business Administration from the Pontifical Catholic University of Peru and a Doctorate in Business Administration from the Maastricht School of Management, the Netherlands. She also has an MPhil from the Maastricht School of Management, the Netherlands and an MBA from the Graduate School of Business Administration, ESAN, in Lima, Peru. She obtained a Bachelor degree in Business Administration and a Bachelor degree in Accounting from the University of the Pacific in Lima, Peru.

Dr Avolio is author of the book *Qualitative Research Methods* (2015); and co-author of the books *Women and Entrepreneurship: Female Durability, Persistence and Intuition at Work* (2014); *Financial Accounting* (2011); *Crisis* (2010); *Rutas Hacia un Perú Mejor, Qué Hacer y Cómo Lograrlo* [*Routes to a Better Peru: What to Do and How to Achieve It*] (2010); *Planeamiento Estratégico para la Gastronomía Peruana* [*Strategic Planning for Peruvian Gastronomy*] (2008); *Cajamarca Competitiva* [*Competitive Cajamarca*] (1998); *Perú: Destino de Inversiones 1997–1998* [*Peru: A Place to Invest 1997–1998*] (1997).

Dr Avolio's doctoral dissertation was entitled 'A Profile of Women Entrepreneurs in Peru: An Exploratory Study'. She is also the author of many academic articles, among others: 'Las limitaciones de la información contable' [The limitations of accounting information] (*Gestión*, 2000); 'Métodos de valorización de empresas' [Methods of company valuation] (*Técnica administrativa*, 2010); and 'Hacia una sociedad de mujeres empresarias' [Towards a society of female entrepreneurs] (*Pathways to a Better Peru*). She has also written articles in newspapers and specialized magazines, including: 'Los Retos de las mujeres emprendedoras' [The challenges of female entrepreneurs] (*Strategia*, 2009);

'Las Mujeres Empresarias en el Perú' [Business women in Peru] (Editorial Norma, forthcoming); and 'Por qué las Mujeres se Convierten en Empresarias' [Why women become entrepreneurs] (CENTRUM Católica 2008).

She is the founder of the Center for Female Entrepreneurs at CENTRUM Católica and is conducting research on female entrepreneurs and executives in Latin America, including the role of female executives in large companies, the role of the entrepreneur's partner and factors that hinder company growth.

Dr Avolio has been a Financial Analyst at Southern Peru Ltd, an international mining company; an Advisor at Price Waterhouse; and Chair of the departments of Finance, Accounting and Economics at various business schools. Her areas of specialization include Finance and Business Management, Financial Planning and Entrepreneurship. Dr Avolio is currently Deputy Director General of CENTRUM Católica and Professor of Finance and Entrepreneurship at CENTRUM Católica.

Preface

We are witnessing a large increase in the production of scientific papers from all research fields. However, many of these scientific papers do not meet the basic criteria in terms of the research methods described, nor in the structure or writing style and the presentation of the results. Moreover, a great number of studies may be considered pointless, since they do not provide any new scientific contribution. In order to avoid all of the above drawbacks, it is necessary to adhere to the research methodology and to follow the approved writing style for scientific papers.

In this book we will, above all, deal with qualitative research methods in economics. The goal is to provide economists with some sort of a road map which they should follow in terms of their methods, either alone or in combination with quantitative methods.

The first part of the book (Chapters 1–6) addresses the role and importance of science, how research in social sciences should be performed, the sources and types of scientific literature, methodology aspects, the design and implementation strategy of qualitative methods, and techniques of data collection.

The second part of the book (Chapters 7–12) offers a detailed, simple, and practical explanation of a research paper based on the qualitative paradigm and applying case study strategy. Several texts address the research methodology from the qualitative and quantitative paradigm perspective, and the methods and concepts for a successful implementation are explained in detail. However, in order to help both master's and doctoral students to develop their own research skills, none of these texts is a complete case study that illustrates how the research method is applied to a particular object of study.

We hope that this book will be sufficiently helpful for its users and that it will encourage them to think about all the necessary steps needed before engaging in a research area. This should be directly reflected in a higher quality of research and in the production of scientific results. Through the achievement of these objectives, the mission of this book would be entirely fulfilled and the efforts of its authors justified.

Acknowledgements

We are grateful to our families and the academic institutions to which we belong – CENTRUM Católica Graduate Business School (Pontificia Universidad Católica del Perú) and Akamai University (United States). This book would not have been possible without their support.

Part I

Applying qualitative methods

Principles and contributions

1 The role and importance of science

The task of science is partly theoretical – explanation – and partly practical – prediction and technical application. I shall try to show that these two aims are, in a way, two different aspects of one and the same activity.

(Popper, 1972, p. 349)

Science must not be sluggish, providing slow solutions, but it simply has to breathe, monitoring and providing quick solutions in response to the challenges facing global society.

(Radović-Marković, 2012, p. 59)

The importance of science for the development of the economy and society

Science, technology and education are directly responsible for the accumulation of new knowledge and they significantly contribute to the development and progress of human life, the economy and society. This is explained by the fact that science, education and technology are recognized as the key drivers of development, bearing in mind that technological and scientific revolutions generate economic progress (Abraham, 2013). The opinion that science and technology contribute to identifying and a better understanding of the problems facing humanity can also be found elsewhere in the literature. Thomas Kuhn (1970) asserts that science should be understood primarily as a social practice, and only then as an intellectual endeavour. Despite this opinion, one cannot ignore the intellectual contribution of scientific workers in creating new knowledge, which has a positive impact on social and economic progress. This was confirmed in the studies that were conducted by the researchers Schofer, Ramirez and Meyer (2000). Namely, they indicated that the number of scientists and the quality of their training have a direct impact on economic development.

Despite these mentioned findings, in many countries the role of science in economic development is not fully respected by the creators of economic and educational policies. Accordingly, in order to increase the benefits from science, it is necessary to take into account a number of factors. These include primarily the following (Watson, *et al.* 2002):

a) Investment in training and human resource development: Human resources are the most important element of science. Consequently, scientific education is the key factor in establishing the scientific capacities of any country or region. The European Commission has emphasized the significance of education for acquiring knowledge, which will contribute to developing the skills of the work force for their active participation in the creation of social wealth: 'What is crucial in the creation of social wealth is that every young person is given the opportunity to use its potential' (European Commission, 2007, p. 2). Therefore, the creators of the scientific policy in a particular country should focus especially on education, considering that education is highly correlated with the development of science.
b) State policies should encourage and provide the environment for strong scientific institutions: Governments should provide greater financial support to create knowledge, from which they would benefit directly.
c) Increasing the level and quality of information and communication technologies that allow the flow and dissemination of knowledge and information: Creators of the state scientific policy in each country should use the media to raise awareness of the importance and the role of science in society.

Although in many countries science has not been given sufficient attention by economic policy creators, there is a wide consensus among scientists that numerous results in the various fields of the social and natural sciences will solve the most persistent problems in the most effective and fastest way.

> This could be also connected to the fact that there is no sustainable economic development without the exchange of new ideas and information, a high level of creativity, and the interaction of science and education with economic subjects through the regional and global scientific network.
>
> (Radović-Marković, 2014, p. 14)

In other words, the development of science in any country not only relies upon the efforts of that nation, but, in addition, the advancement is influenced by international scientific collaboration. With this in mind, it can be concluded that international scientific collaboration represents an important component of a society's orientation towards the development of scientific achievements. Accordingly, scientific institutions are responsible for raising awareness in a society of the role and value of science. Directly related to this statement, a question arises regarding the new possibilities and modalities of scientific communication that would contribute to improving the dissemination of research results, and thus increase the return of investment in research and development (Radović-Marković, 2014).

Social sciences versus natural sciences

Social sciences deal with the individual or collective behaviour of people or groups of people, companies, economies and societies. They try to determine the existing cause and effect relationships among phenomena in an objective manner, both in specific areas of social life, as well as in society as a whole of all social relations. 'These sciences can be classified into disciplines such as psychology, the science of human behavior, sociology, the science of social groups, and economy, the science of companies, markets and economies' (Bhattacherjee, 2012, p. 1). Unlike the social sciences, the natural sciences deal with the examination of natural phenomena, such as matter, the earth, heavenly bodies, or the human body (physics, chemistry, astronomy, medicine, etc.).

There is a significant difference between the natural and social sciences. While in the natural sciences there are certain patterns of relations that occur with such regularity that they are considered principles, such principles do not exist in the social sciences. Namely, unlike the natural sciences that seek universal laws of natural phenomena within nature, the practical application of theoretical models is of particular relevance to the social sciences. This is consistent with the opinion of Adam Smith, the founder of economics, who considered himself more of a philosopher who is constantly looking for opportunities to achieve the prosperity and well-being of people, than a scientist in search of universal economic laws (Jacobs, *et al.*, 2014).

Each of the social sciences, with some minor exceptions, attempts to understand and explain certain aspects of social reality. Economics is sometimes celebrated as the queen of the social sciences, acting as a promoter and driver of the other social sciences (Duhs, 2006). In economic literature, the idea that the economic sciences should follow the other scientific disciplines in their development can often be identified. This primarily refers to the natural sciences and their principles of development.

Theoretical postulates of science

A theory can be defined as a general and, more or less, comprehensive set of statements that describe different aspects of a phenomenon (Babbie, 1998; Hagan, 1993; Senese, 1997). A theory may also represent an attempt to provide an explanation about reality, or provide a way for classifying and describing events and even predict the future of an event (Hagan, 1993).

Each theory consists of the following elements (Radović, 1996):

a) a series of definitions that explain the variables used in a precise manner;
b) a number of assumptions that provide a brief description of the conditions under which a certain theory is applied;
c) one or more hypotheses that are derived from the assumptions on which the theory is based;
d) the hypotheses that can be tested using different techniques.

'The main purpose of any theory consists in the fact that it should demonstrate how different things are associated with one another' (Radović, 1996, p. 161). Namely, if one knows what kind of relation is established between the two variables, one can easily find out how one of them will change with the change of the other.

Assumptions also play an important role in the formation of a theory. They most often involve the form of describing and presenting a theory. 'They can also serve as an indirect test of hypotheses, and they are sometimes in the function of determining the conditions under which a particular theory is expected to be valid' (Radović, 1996, p. 162).

The economic theory

A theory indicates which parameters are important and how they can be measured. 'Economics was studied for many years as a theoretical discipline, which was based on a set of qualitative analyses and definitions' (Radović, 1996, p. 151). However, in order to be able to follow the requirements with which it was faced under the influence of constant changes in the socio-economic environment, economics had to evolve throughout its history and change its development model. This has consequently led to the quantification of economic theory, and as a result the descriptive and historical orientation in economic science gave way to the formalist approach (Radović, 1996). Therefore, nowadays, there is almost no area of research in which quantitative methods and techniques are not present, used either alone or in combination with qualitative methods, thanks to which they can provide answers to a number of theoretical and practical questions. Thus, for example, the Laffer curve shows the relationship between tax rates and tax revenues. The scientist Laffer, after which the curve was named, believed that high tax rates represent the main culprits for the existence of low national savings, low investment and recession. The tax rates are applied to the abscissa, while the tax revenues, which are realized through the application of appropriate tax rates, are assigned to the ordinate. 'The popularity of the Laffer curve is a result of the fact that you can explain it to anyone in six minutes and then you can talk about it for six months' (Varian, 1989, p. 4). We have taken it as an example bearing in mind that the Laffer analysis indicates the good and bad sides of an economic theory. The downside of this theory can be seen in the fact that what this theory predicts may happen in real life, but not necessarily.

In many cases, the practice has proved this theory wrong. 'Following the reduction in tax rates, tax revenues did not increase, what's more they decreased, which contributed to an increase in the budget deficit' (Kulić, 2009, p. 46). The positive side of this theory is that it refers to the use of a simple analysis. In addition, it emphasizes the relevant parameters for drawing conclusions, which we would not be able to discern without this theory. Considering that the purpose of every theory is to explain some phenomenon, it often represents a certain abstraction, simplification or generalization, and as such generally has characteristics of a hypothesis. 'Namely, if practice confirms a hypothesis, in that case the hypothesis turns into a scientific theory' (Radović, 1996, p. 152).

Krugman (2013) argues that an economic theory consists of numerous mathematical models that vary in their complexity. Furthermore, Krugman emphasizes the fact that they are all incomplete; that is, they leave out some of the most important features of their objectives. Many of them are incompatible, as they illuminate various goals with many simplifications that make them inaccurate because of their idealizations. Friedman (1953) believed that good economic theories are those that can provide accurate and useful predictions, while Samuelson (1947) pointed out that economists should formulate theories based on a 'practical concept'. In this way, the theories are ideally a logical equivalent to their described characteristics. It should also be noted that in contrast to the exact sciences, there are great difficulties in providing an assessment of the validity of a particular theory within the economic sciences, 'given that there is still no agreed standard for the refutation of hypotheses, which underlie any theory' (Radović-Marković, 2015, p. 3).

In recent years, the economic theory has found itself, more than ever before, at the point of its own review under the influence of major financial crisis. This is reflected in the numerous debates among economic experts who have questioned the new Keynesian theory and the views of its main follower Minsky, as well as modern monetary theory and the Austrian school of economics. This can be considered fully justified, bearing in mind that when an economic crisis occurs, economic theory is also in crisis, a fact that was recognized by Joanna Robinson decades ago (Robinson, 1981).

An economic philosophy as the basis of economic theory

'From the very beginning, economics has sought to break away from emotions and to fight for the status of science' (Robinson, 1962, p. 35). Chronologically speaking, the initial use of philosophy in economics can be attached to the names of John Stuart Mill and William Whewell, whose works paved the way in the nineteenth century when they were created for the further development of economic philosophy. In the late nineteenth and early twentieth century, logical positivism occurred, which is associated with the 'formalist revolution' in economics (Radović, 1996, p. 151). This is when the question of the relationship between scientific theories and scientific principles was set as a general problem for the first time.

The role of economic philosophy was particularly emphasized by Heilbroner (1996), which is reflected in its importance for determining its contribution to social welfare.

Prominent economists such as Robinson, Myrdal, Higgins, and Heilbroner felt that economic philosophy was of crucial importance and that it represented the basis for the establishment of economic theory. Therefore, the comprehension of economic philosophy, which an economic theory is based upon, represented a prerequisite for understanding many controversies in economic science. In addition, there was also an increasing need for establishing relations between 'pure theory' and 'applied theory', as well as for the delimitation of those theories that can be tested from those theories whose postulates cannot be tested and proven by means of different methodological instruments. The objectivity of science is based on the constant verification of theories in practice. Therefore, the corpus of science consists at any one moment of the theories that have not been disproved (Robinson, 1962). Namely, the successfulness of a theory is measured by the ability of an exact prediction of a particular phenomenon with the possibility of controlling this phenomenon. However, the design and testing of theories is particularly difficult in economics and the other social sciences, owing to the insufficient accuracy of theoretical concepts and inadequate instruments for their testing. In addition, it is very difficult to refute the theories that 'do not work'. For example, Marx's theory persisted for several decades in the socialist bloc countries before being discredited as inefficient in terms of stimulating economic growth and social welfare.

The above mentioned example and other similar examples show that, unlike the theories in the natural sciences, the theories in the social sciences are rarely perfect, which offers many opportunities for researchers to improve these theories, or to build their own new alternative theories.

Science versus pseudoscience

> When the science does not change in accordance with the experimental evidences, it becomes a pseudoscience.
>
> (Hill, 2010)

The determination of the boundaries between science and pseudoscience has caused much disagreement in scientific circles. The famous scientist Karl Popper was the first to identify that limit. Namely, he defined the criteria for distinguishing an empirical science, such as Einstein's theory of relativity, from a pseudoscience in which he ranked Freud's theory. However, Freud's theory was difficult to refute as it is not possible to test its hypotheses, as they were not openly set. Thus, Popper proclaimed 'the inability to test a certain theory and determine its inaccuracy' as the border of demarcation (Hill, 2010).

One of the criteria that encountered general applicability in the demarcation of a science from a pseudoscience refers to the appreciation for everything that contributes to the constitution of a particular science. This implies a set of methods aimed at testing hypotheses and theories, whose aim is the creation of scientific knowledge. If a community of scientists actively adopts new ideas and if these ideas are incorporated into research, then useful knowledge is produced and we can talk about science (Shermer, 2011) (Figure 1.1). In accordance with this opinion, it can be concluded that scientific knowledge is related to those general laws and theories that explain phenomena or behaviour by means of scientific methods.

Unlike scientists who reject a theory that has not been confirmed by experiments, pseudoscientists do not recognize the results of experiments unless they confirm their theory. Therein lays the essence of bad science and pseudoscience (Figure 1.2).

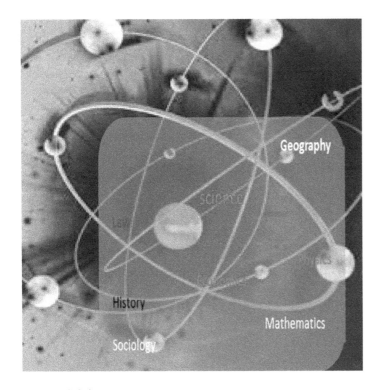

Figure 1.1 Science

Figure 1.2 Pseudoscience

Although it seems that the criteria are very clear and precise in distinguishing science from pseudoscience, different opinions can be found in the recent literature. Thus, the scientist Pigliucci (2010) argued in his book *Nonsense on Stilts* that the boundaries between science and pseudoscience are looser than many scientists want to believe. Namely, when we talk about medicine, physics and biology, the scientific value of a particular theory is generally apparent. However, there are numerous examples of 'sciences' whose scientific value is masked and presented as legitimate science, which creates confusion in the academic community. An example of such a science is homeopathy, which has 'evidences', but relies entirely on inaccurate conclusions derived from them (Hill, 2010). In addition to the above-mentioned example, similar examples can be found in other areas as well (astrology, hypnosis, etc.).

Exercise

1   Analyse the role of science in economic development.
2   Explain the basic purpose of any theory.
3   Discuss the importance of understanding an economic philosophy.
4   Make a distinction between science and pseudoscience.
5   Find several websites on the Internet where pseudoscience is presented.

References

Abraham, J. (2013). *Economic benefits of science and technology development.* Available at: http://www.punchng.com/business/am-business/economic-benefits-of-science-and-technology-development/

Babbie, E. (1998). *The Practice of Social Research* (8th edition). Belmont, CA: Wadsworth Publishing.

Bhattacherjee, A. (2012). *Social Science Research: Principles, Methods, and Practices* (2nd edition). Florida: Creative Commons Attribution.

Duhs, L. A. (2006). Is economic philosophy a subject worth teaching? *Australasian Journal of Economics Education,* 3(1/2), 90–110.

European Commission (2007). Communication from the Commission to the Council, the European Parliament, the Economic and Social Committee and the Committee of the Regions: 'Promoting young people's full participation in education, employment and society'. COM(2007) 498 final. Brussels. Available at: http://ec.europa.eu/employment_social/employment_strategy/pdf/youthcom_2007_en.pdf

Friedman, M. (1953). The methodology of positive economics. In: *The Methodology of Positive Economics.* Chicago: University of Chicago Press, pp. 3–43.

Hagan, F. E. (1993). *Research Methods in Criminal Justice and Criminology* (3rd edition). New York: Macmillan.

Heilbroner, R. (1996).The embarrassment of economics. *Challenge,* (November/December), 46–49.

Hill, K. (2010). *The difference between science and pseudoscience*. Available at: https://sciencebasedlife.wordpress.com/2010/12/03/the-difference-between-science-and-psuedoscience/

Jacobs, J., Nagan, W. and Zucconi, A. (2014). Unification in the social sciences: Search for a science of society. *Cadmus*, 2(3), 1–22.

Krugman, P. (2013). *End This Depression Now*. New York: W. W. Norton & Company.

Kuhn, T. (1970). *The Structure of Scientific Revolutions*. Chicago: University of Chicago Press.

Kulić, M. (2009). Finansijska i ekonomska načela oporezivanja [Financial and economic principles of taxation], *Škola biznisa* [*School of Business*]. Available at: http://www.vps.ns.ac.rs/SB/2009/2.6.pdf

Pigliucci, M. (2010). *Nonsense on Stilts*. Chicago: University of Chicago Press.

Popper, K. (1972). *Objective Knowledge: An Evolutionary Approach*. Oxford: Clarendon Press.

Radović, M. (1996). Ekonomska analiza na novim (kvantitativnim) osnovama [Economic analysis on new (quantitative basis)]. In: R. Aničić (Ed.) *Uvod u metode ekonomske analize-teorijsko filozofske osnove naučnog metoda* [*Introduction to the Method of Economic Analysis and Theoretical Philosophical Underpinnings of the Scientific Method*]. Faculty of Economics, University of Belgrade.

Radović-Marković, M. (2012). Creative education and new learning as means of encouraging creativity, original thinking and entrepreneurship. In: *Humanities and the Contemporary World*. Montenegrin Academy of Sciences and Arts, Podgorica, Montenegro.

Radović-Marković, M. (2014). Uloga akademija nauka u razmeni naučnih znanja i iskustava u cilju podsticanja društveno-ekonomskog razvoja zemalja zapadnog Balkana [The role of the academies of science in the exchange of scientific knowledge and experience for the purpose of enhancing the socio-economic development of the Western Balkan countries]. Academy of Sciences and Arts of the Republic of Srpska (ANURS), Banja Luka, Bosnia and Herzegovina, Invited lecture, September 2014.

Radović-Marković, M. (2015).The limits of the scientific method in economics and business: A critical view. *Economic Analysis*, 48(3/4), 1–8.

Robinson, J. (1962). *Economic Philosophy*. London: Watts.

Robinson, J. (1981). *Ekonomska filozofija* [*Economic Philosophy*]. Belgrade: Istraživačko-izdavački centar SSO Srbije [Research and Publishing Centre SSO Srbije].

Samuelson, P. A. (1947). *Foundations of Economic Analysis*. Cambridge, MA: Harvard University Press.

Schofer, E., Ramirez, F. and Meyer, J. (2000). The effects of science on national economic development, 1970–1990. *American Sociological Review*, 65, 877–898.

Senese, J. D. (1997). *Applied Research Methods in Criminal Justice*. Chicago: Nelson-Hall.

Shermer, M. (2011). What Is Pseudoscience? *Scientific American*, 1 September.

Varian, H. (1989). *Handbook of Industrial Organization, Vol. 1*. Amsterdam: North-Holland, pp. 597–654.

Watson, R., Crawford, M. and Farley, S. (2002). *Strategic Approaches to Science and Technology in Development*. World Bank, Washington, DC. Available at: http://sitere sources.worldbank.org/EDUCATION/Resources/278200-,1089743700155/content.pdf

2   Research in the social sciences

What is being examined in the social sciences is not merely the nature that blindly follows the laws of nature, but the freedom as the basis of active life and the key assumption of its meaning and value.

(Babić, 2012, p. 1)

Why do we perform research in the social sciences?

Our perceptions of social phenomena are necessarily limited, considering that we as individuals have our own notions based mainly on our own common-sense knowledge. However, this does not give us a reliable basis for understanding these phenomena.

As common-sense knowledge is not scientifically based, scientific methods for the research of social phenomena are required, for which social surveys provide us with the tools. Therefore, research in the social sciences includes social scientific methods, theories and concepts that can improve our understanding of social processes and problems. This research is conducted by economists, sociologists, political scientists, psychologists and anthropologists.

The notion and characteristics of research

We all possess the vital instinct of a curiosity aimed at comprehending and understanding better a particular phenomenon, problem or process that is unknown to us. This curiosity is the mother of all knowledge and the methods that men use for acquiring knowledge can be rightly called the research.

The aim of scientific research is to learn new facts, test ideas, and discover something new that contributes to a certain scientific discipline. Namely, it is the systematic collection, analysis and interpretation of data in order to generate new knowledge, as well as to provide answers to specific questions.

Any research requires taking the following steps:

a)   clearly defining the subject of research;
b)   setting up the plan of research;
c)   literature review and the use of existing research results;
d)   collection of new data that could answer the research questions.

Types of research

Research is a systematic search for information and new knowledge (Degu and Yigzaw, 2006). It covers topics in every field of science. Research can be classified as:

> *Applied research:* In applied research, scientific knowledge is put into practice. The researcher is interested in contributing to the overall progress of a particular field in a practical sense.
> *Quantitative research:* Dealing with the response to the following questions: How many? How often? To what extent?
> *Qualitative research:* Engaged in finding answers to the questions that begin with: Why? How? In which way?

We can also differentiate research that aims at showing that consideration of particular phenomena can be subsumed under the laws of nature, and research that seeks to increase and deepen the existing knowledge about events, processes or phenomena (Hermerén, 2011).

Research objectives

The purpose of research is to discover answers to many questions throughout the application of scientific procedures. The main aim of research is to find out the truth that is hidden and which has not been discovered as yet (Kothari, 2004).

Although each study has its own particular purpose, research objectives can be grouped into:

a) those that contribute to familiarizing with a particular phenomenon or acquiring new insights;
b) those that serve to illustrate the characteristics of an individual, situation or a group (studies with this aim are known as descriptive research);
c) those that follow and determine the frequency with which certain phenomenon occurs;
d) those that are used to test hypotheses and determine the causal relationships between variables.

The criteria for determining the subject of research

In selecting the subject of research, it is necessary to adhere to the following criteria:

a) The importance of the problem: To what extent is this problem important for individuals and society?
b) Avoidance of duplication: To what extent has this problem been studied before? Are there any answers that have not been provided on the main issues, which deserve further research?

c) Feasibility of the research: Do we have all the necessary resources (human and financial) to conduct the research?
d) Applicability of possible results and recommendations: What is the probability of applying the recommendations from the study?
e) Ethical acceptability: It should be considered whether our research could harm others.

Research phases

Research includes the following stages:

a) review and evaluation of the literature;
b) formulation of the research questions;
c) choice of methodology and formulation of the hypotheses;
d) data collection;
e) data analysis;
f) drawing conclusions;
g) understanding the limitations of research;
h) recommendations for further work.

When should you not conduct research?

You should not conduct a research when:

a) you know the answer in advance;
b) the answer is irrelevant (scientifically or practically);
c) you do not have all the necessary resources (financial, human, technical, etc).

Common characteristics of successful research

Although each research is different, the following factors are common to all good research papers:

a) There is a clear definition of the research objectives.
b) There is a research draft that clearly defines what the research is about, what it will involve and the methodologies used in accordance with the research questions.
c) A good researcher can use a combination of methodologies, which complement each other.
d) The research should be conducted in an impartial manner.
e) As far as possible, the researcher should not influence the research results.
f) From the very beginning of the research, the researcher should have adequate and sufficient human, financial and other resources.
g) All researches must be ethical; that is, they should not be harmful in any way for the research participants.

The main qualities of a successful researcher

Every good researcher should possess the appropriate level of theoretical knowledge, be patient and persistent in his/her intentions and have the capacity for logical and critical thinking. Logical and critical thinking are especially important in order to be able to:

a) *Properly evaluate sources of information:* The ability to choose the most reliable and accurate source in relation to a given topic from alternative sources (e.g. to be able to distinguish between primary and secondary sources).

b) *Separate facts from opinions:* The ability to make a basic distinction between facts (those that can be proved or confirmed empirically) and opinions (those that cannot be proved or confirmed).

c) *Recognize stereotypes:* The ability to identify simplified and exaggerated descriptions of people and their behaviour that are based on racial, religious or other grounds. They are most often the result of misinformation or the lack of good information.

d) *Have the ability to empathize with others:* The ability to perceive a particular situation from the perspective of the other person is an important skill. This helps to consider a problem in a way that has not been taken into account earlier.

e) *Be familiar with the research techniques:* A person who is not well informed can never be a successful researcher. It is particularly important to be familiar with the research techniques without which the research cannot be performed.

f) *Be very interested in the area in which the research shall be conducted:* The researcher needs to be devoted to research tasks. Furthermore, he/she should allocate sufficient time for these tasks. However, in addition to a good theoretical background for the implementation of scientific research, researchers are also required to possess methodological skills and knowledge.

Exercise

1   To invest in research implies investing in a better future for every nation. Does that statement sound true? Justify your answer.
2   Why is cooperation in scientific research important?
3   Why do we need to analyse the research problem?
4   What do we need to focus on in order to justify the selected research problem?

References

Babić, J. (2012). *Applied Ethics in European Union* (in cooperation with Dr Ilija Vujačić). Applied Ethics series, Službeni Glasnik [Official Gazette].
Degu, G. and Yigzaw, T. (2006). *Research Methodology*. Ethiopia Ministry of Education, Addis Ababa.
Hermerén, G. (2011). *Good Research Practice*. Swedish Research Council, Stockholm.
Kothari, C. R. (2004). *Research Methodology: Methods & Techniques*. New Delhi: New Age International (P) Ltd.

3 Sources and types of scientific literature

The literature of a scientific specialty area is the accumulated corpus of research articles, and it is regarded as the primary repository of knowledge that defines the state of that field.

(Holmes, 1987, p.224)

The importance of scientific literature

Having access to the scientific literature is critical for scientific work. The reason why access to the literature is so important lies in the fact that it is a reliable archive of scientific research. Digital and online databases make it easier for scientists to search the literature. However, access to most journals is limited by subscription. As a result, scientific institutions without the resources to pay for these subscriptions are disadvantaged (Evans and Reimer, 2009). More recently, many journals are providing open access to their contents after a certain period of time, as in the case of the journal *Science*, and some offer open access from the very beginning (*Economic Analysis*, *Journal of Women's Entrepreneurship and Education*, *International Review*, etc.). This change reflects awareness that a diversity of viewpoints improves our scientific understanding, and that anyone who is interested in science should have free access to scientific literature.

The scientific literature includes thousands of journals and hundreds of thousands of books. In order to search this vast scientific literature, the researchers are required to possess knowledge that can be learned primarily through experience. Namely, the researcher can access the scientific literature relatively easily when he/she possesses the necessary skills and is aware of the strategies that can be used. Above all, one needs to know how to make a distinction between scientific literature and other literature (popular, professional, etc.) and how to distinguish the main sources of scientific information in terms of their quality.

What is the scientific literature?

Scientists communicate and share their findings with other scientists primarily through the scientific literature. The scientific literature represents a permanent repository of scientific knowledge and a record of progress in scientific research.

Proper use of literature

Proper use of literature enables us to:

a) avoid duplicating the work that someone else has done before;
b) cover the knowledge of the problem that we want to explore;
c) get acquainted with different research methods.

The following sources of scientific information should be used with 'extreme caution' as a part of scientific research:

a) *Newspapers:* Newspapers do not publish scientific articles. Therefore, they are not considered part of the scientific literature. However, they can be used with caution in the social sciences for very specific needs.
b) *Scientific magazines:* Usually, they are popularly written and do not rely upon original research.
c) *The Internet:* An abundance of information relating to economic sciences, as well as to other scientific disciplines, can be found on the Internet. This information ranges from absolute scientific falsehoods to material of high quality. However, the professional look of the website does not always guarantee the quality of information: there are high-quality websites that offer the entirely wrong information. On the other hand, there are peer-reviewed scientific journals that are published on the Internet. Internet users should be very careful when evaluating the source, quality and accuracy of information they plan to use.

Sources of information

a) Published information (books, journals, etc.);
b) unpublished documents (studies in related fields, reports, etc.);
c) opinions, certificates of authority to practice a profession.

Types of literature

Owing to the great abundance of literature in the field of economics, finding the desired information requires resourcefulness. Therefore, it is necessary to possess a broad knowledge of the different types of literature and the ways in which to search for it. To help obtain the required information more easily and efficiently, note that the overall economic literature can be classified into several groups:

a) *primary literature* – includes published original scientific papers issued in scientific journals;
b) *secondary literature* – contains extracts from reference works; that is, primary literature (textbooks, manuals, etc.);

c)   *tertiary literature* – made up of sources that consist of information collected from primary and secondary sources (yearbooks, bibliographies, dictionaries and encyclopedias, etc.);

d)   *grey literature* – includes government documents, special online publications and similar literature.

Primary (basic) literature

Primary literature refers to those papers in which the research of individual scientists, or that made by the collaboration of a group of scientists, is published. These papers are published in a peer-reviewed scientific journal. These journals usually prescribe a form of scientific paper, which should be prepared in accordance with technical instructions.

Papers presented at international, regional or national conferences, workshops and symposia are considered as primary sources of literature if they are peer-reviewed and published either in the form of conference proceedings, or in a special issue of a scientific journal. On the other hand, abstracts of papers presented at a conference, or the papers themselves, which have not been peer-reviewed, do not count as primary literature even if they are published in book form.

It is especially important to emphasize that academic research is based on primary sources. Some examples of primary sources of literature are:

a)   Research Papers in Economics (RePEc): http://ideas.repec.org (it also has links to published journal articles)

b)   Social Science Research Network (SSRN): http://papers.ssrn.com

c)   Sciencedirect: http://www.sciencedirect.com

d)   http://www.ien.bg.ac.rs/index.php/sr/asopis-ekon-analiza

e)   http://www.ien.bg.ac.rs/index.php/sr/asopis-preduzetnitvo.

Secondary literature

Secondary literature consists of works that rely on primary sources of information. The purpose of these works is to demonstrate synthesized knowledge in a particular scientific field.

This type of literature includes monographs, textbooks and manuals. Although these works are written in a scientific style, secondary publications are not organized in the same manner as the primary publications. Scientists use secondary literature in order to familiarize themselves with existing research, or to obtain information about new topics on which they plan to start working. Some examples of secondary sources of literature are:

a)   Google: http://scholar.google.com

b)   Resources for Economists: http://www.rfe.org/

c)   http://www.amazon.co.uk/Books-Mirjana-RadovicMarkovic/s?ie=UTF8& page=1&rh=n%3A266239%2Cp_27%3AMirjana%20Radovic-Markovic.

Tertiary literature

Tertiary literature consists of published papers that are based on primary or secondary sources of literature. Such papers are written in a more informal style than the scientific papers. They may also contain a short biography of the author, but do not include a list of references.

The tertiary literature includes newsletters, articles in newspapers, science magazines and encyclopedias. Some examples of tertiary sources of literature are:

a)   *The Economist*: http://www.economist.com
b)   *The New York Times*: http://www.nytimes.com
c)   *The Wall Street Journal*: http://www.wsj.com.

'Grey' literature

Grey literature refers to sources of scientific information that are not published and distributed in the usual manner, and because of this they may be difficult to obtain. It includes: papers and dissertations, technical reports with a limited distribution, journals issued by special interest groups, abstracts from congresses and conferences (collections of abstracts) that are only available to conference participants, some types of government documents, and certain online documents.

It should be noted that 'grey literature' is not without scientific value. The problem with grey literature mainly refers to its limited distribution and difficulties related to its availability.

Basic steps of a scientific literature search

When searching the scientific literature one should take the following steps:

a)   Use encyclopedias, textbooks or other readily available sources.
b)   Create an initial list of 'key words' which can be used to explore a specific topic.
c)   Browse the electronic catalog. The Internet should be used for bibliographic research as it saves a lot of time when searching for references. An exhaustive database of scientific data can be accessed over the Internet through various channels, including key words, names of authors and titles of papers. Many databases provide only abstracts, while a relatively small number of journals publish complete articles online that can be accessed without a subscription.

Usefulness of a good literature selection

A good selection of literature:

a)   indicates that you are familiar with the subject matter;
b)   confirms the objectives of your research;
c)   allows you to create a theoretical framework and to have a good methodological focus on the research.

Points for discussion

1 Are the tertiary sources of literature acceptable in academic papers? Explain why or why not?
2 Find an example of one primary, secondary and tertiary source of literature on the Internet and provide links.

References

Evans, J. A. and Reimer, J. (2009). Open access and global participation in science. *Science*, 323(5917), 1025.
Holmes, F. L. (1987). Scientific writing and scientific discovery. *Isis*, 78, 220–235.

4   Methodology and research methods

> What methodology can do is to set the criteria for the acceptance and rejection of research programs by setting standards. These standards are hierarchical, relative, dynamic, and by no means unambiguous in the practical advice they offer to working economists.
>
> (Blaug, 1980, p. 264)

> The scientific method is a kind of elephant; this is something that can be described, which exists, but cannot be defined.
>
> (Robinson, 1962, p.25)

The notion of methodology

Methodology (from Greek *methodos* – path, way of gaining knowledge, *logos* – science) represents a branch of logic that deals with the validity of applying scientific methods in the individual concrete sciences.

Every science should adhere to certain general methodological procedures and principles. In this sense, the general logical and methodological rules apply equally to all sciences.

Methodological aspects

Methodology pays particular attention to logical, technical, organizational and strategic aspects:

a) Logical aspects include all the rules related to defining concepts, constructing definitions, creating classifications and typologies, drawing conclusions and evidences, as well as the procedures referring to the hypotheses and theories testing.
b) Technical aspects imply the use of all those special techniques by which science seeks to acquire knowledge (observation, interview, survey, experiment, comparison, use of statistics, use of historical sources, etc.).
c) Organizational aspects refer to those methodological rules that include the most optimal organizational forms of scientific work, the communication and

exchange of experiences among researchers, and the teamwork skills in the process of research, etc.

d)   Strategic aspects relate to setting clear long-term theoretical objectives and the realization of practical conditions for their achievement.

Scientific methods

For a clear perception of the term research, one must comprehend the meaning of the scientific method. The two terms, research and scientific method, are closely related. Scientific methods and techniques are the common feature of all research, although they may vary considerably from one science to another. 'Scientific method is the pursuit of truth through logical considerations, i.e. it attempts to achieve an ideal combination of experimentation, observation, logical arguments' (Ostle and Mensing, 1975, p. 2). 'Scientific method refers to a standardized set of techniques for building scientific knowledge, such as how to make valid observations, how to interpret results, and how to generalize those results' (Bhattacherjee, 2012, p. 5). The scientific method should meet four criteria:

a)   *Replicability:* This criterion implies the possibility of repeating a scientific study and obtaining similar, if not identical, results.
b)   *Precision:* Theoretical concepts must be defined with such precision that others can also use them as definitions for measuring those concepts and test theories.
c)   *Verifiability:* A theory must be stated in a way that it can be tested. Theories that cannot be tested are not considered scientific theories.
d)   *Simplicity:* When there are several explanations of a phenomenon, scientists must always accept the simplest and the most logical explanation.

Both the natural and social sciences have in common the fact that they are based on the same logic of the scientific method. Truthfulness is proved empirically, and the empirical method is based on its practical applicability in society.

The use of the scientific method is the most important tool in the study of the social sciences, as it allows us not only to learn lessons from certain social sciences, but also to understand their synthesis as well (Figure 4.1).

The limitations of the scientific method in economics and business

Despite the fact that the scientific method has found great applicability in economics and business, its possibilities are very limited when predicting future economic developments. This opinion was confirmed by the French philosopher Peirce, who concluded that no new ideas have been derived from analysis of the past with the help of inductive and deductive logic, the two forms of logic used in modern scientific methods (Martin, 2011). Some predictions have recently proved to be completely wrong. However, starting from the fact that any kind of

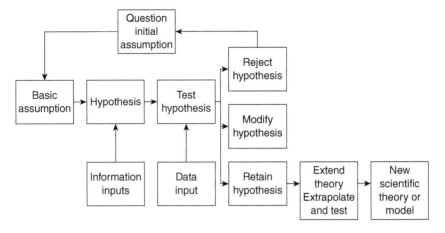

Figure 4.1 Steps in the scientific method (source: http://www.pixbam.com/steps-of-the-scientific-method/the-6-steps-of-the-scientific/110413)

prediction is better than nothing at all, governments of modern states and large corporations insist on the projections of conjectural developments. They are dealing with predictions of employment rates, inflation rates and the increase or decrease in the gross domestic product; almost every aspect of strategic enterprise management refers to the future: from planning the production of goods and sales to business expansion, or the opening of a new organization. Nevertheless, these future predictions by economists have long been very limited in certain segments, given that some aspects related to other social sciences were not taken into account. However, in recent years, things are beginning to change owing to those scientists who are bringing down the barriers between scientific disciplines (Ioannides and Nielsen, 2007; Poli, 2014).

Accordingly, the possibilities of anticipation from climate change to economic crisis are discussed in scientific circles. Predictions are particularly associated with a high degree of risk of their failure to comply in a time of economic crisis. The problem lies in the fact that

> in terms of fundamental uncertainty, the expectations cannot be understood as a result of the calculated optimal choice, taking into account all available information, but are based on the potential interpretation of a situation in the context of prevailing institutional structures, cultural patterns and social network.
>
> (Beckert, 2013, p. 325)

These considerations are bringing together researchers from different scientific disciplines, with the aim of establishing an interdisciplinary dialogue that should serve as a basis for understanding and creating the policy of future decision-making. A better and more complete understanding of future trends and their effects will improve theories and models in economics and the other social sciences. These improvements will greatly benefit those who explicitly seek to create a 'ready society'. In this way, modern technologies will be used more efficiently and the limits of human endeavour will be explored (Poli, 2014); in addition, the response to the challenges of global society will improve.

The difference between methodologies and methods

Although there are a number of scientific disciplines, and within them an even greater number of different types of research, the methodology has, as a universal science (i.e. metamethodology), defined certain standards and rules that apply to each scientific project and each scientific research. However, the method is a way of research that is being applied in a particular science. Namely, the method of a certain science is the way this science observes or investigates the phenomena and processes that are important for the object of study.

During their existence, the social sciences have demonstrated a much greater number of problems and contradictory relations between their theories and empirical facts than the natural sciences. These significant differences arise primarily from the diversity of the very objects of study, but they also stem from the differences in methodological possibilities. The social sciences cannot use the methods and research procedures of the natural sciences to the same extent and in the same scope. This particularly refers to the most frequently used and most reliable experimental methods. There are clear ethical and methodological limits in the application of experiments in the social sciences.

The classification of scientific methods

Within the literature, the systematization of scientific methods is most often done in several groups:

a) *basic methods:* these involve analysis, synthesis, abstraction, concretization, specialization, generalization, deduction, induction, etc.;
b) *special methods:* the most important include positivism, historicism and the dialectic method;
c) *general scientific methods* (these are applied or can be applied in all the sciences): they include statistical methods, axiomatic methods, modelling methods and comparative methods;
d) *methods of data collection:* the following stand out: test methods, methods of observation, experiment methods, method of document analysis and case study methods;
e) *methods of data processing:* these represent the modalities of the application of general scientific methods or their extensions.

Basic methods

The most frequently applied methods of scientific research are:

a) inductive and deductive methods

    i) methods of description
    ii) analysis and synthesis
    iii) abstraction
    iv) compilation
    v) methods of proving and refuting.

Inductive and deductive methods

When we observe the scientific process, it is difficult to separate induction – reasoning from experience – and deduction – logical derivation of consequences from the assumptions formulated in the form of universal (general) statements.

In the opinion of certain scientists, induction and deduction have a common basic subject of knowledge, which is accessed by integrating both methods (Primorac, 2010). Therefore, it is difficult to make a sharp distinction between induction and deduction in qualitative research. Thus, in research using inductive methods, the aim of a researcher is to form theoretical concepts on the basis of obtained data and the results. On the other hand, in those studies which are based on deductive methods, the goal of researchers is to test concepts and patterns that are known from the theory using new empirical data. Bearing this in mind, inductive methods are otherwise known as methods for formulating new theories, while deductive methods are seen as methods for testing existing theories. The aim of testing a theory is not only to verify its validity and reliability, but also to offer its possible improvement. Furthermore, it should be taken into account that both methods are of equal importance for the advancement of science.

Unlike traditional empirical studies, qualitative research emphasizes the induction method as a primary method of cognition (Primorac, 2010). The inductive method involves the systematic application of inductive reasoning, wherein one comes to general conclusions based on the analysis of individual facts. Within the inductive approach, a theory is not a starting point in research, but may be developed as a result of research. Therefore, the inductive method is otherwise known as the 'bottom-up' approach, while the deductive method is often informally called the 'top-down' approach.

Another name for valid reasoning is deductive reasoning. Hempel and Oppenheim (1965) were the first to come to the conclusion that all scientific explanations have a common logical structure: they are given with the help of deductive logic.

This method represents the use of a deductive method of reasoning, wherein the unique and specific conclusions are drawn from general judgements. In accordance with the rules of deductive logic, this means the infallible syllogistic

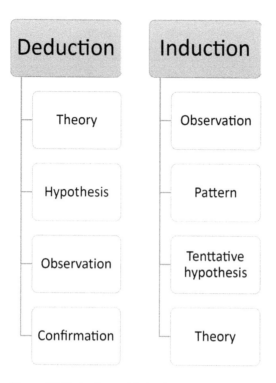

Figure 4.2 Deduction and induction

reasoning as: all A are B, all C are A → all C are B, whereas it really 'cannot' happen that the conclusion is false if the premises are true. The reasoning is, hence, the process in which, by following the rules of thinking, one starts from a group of viewpoints and ends with a new viewpoint. The deductive method deals with testing and confirming hypotheses.

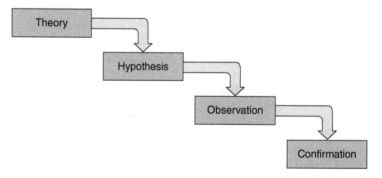

Figure 4.3 The deductive method (source: http://www. socialresearchmethods. net/kb/ dedind.php)

The most important elements of the deductive method are the following procedures: analysis, synthesis, generalization, abstraction, proving and compilation.

a) The method of analysis is the process of scientific research in which complex concepts are broken down into their simpler component parts. The general object of analysis is always a complex whole, which cannot have less than two interrelated parts. The whole and its parts have their own spatial and temporal characteristics, their qualitative and quantitative features and properties, composition, external and internal relations and relationships, movements, changes, development, etc. There are two types of analysis: descriptive (when the elements of the whole are described) and explicative (when the whole is explained based on its parts).

b) The method of synthesis is the process of scientific research wherein the understanding of a complex whole is done by placing their individual and specific parts in various possible relations and relationships. Subjects of synthesis may include concepts, attitudes, judgements, conclusions, etc.

c) The method of generalization is the thought process of generalization, which implies that by starting from one particular notion one can reach a more general notion that is at a higher level than any other (Kulenović, 2005). The basic concepts of generalization, which are essential for quantitative research, are now being applied to a certain extent in qualitative research as well. 'The generalization of research results is not established upon the final analysis, but rather by the induction that begins on the individual case' (Primorac, 2010, p. 23).

d) Abstraction is one of the basic methods of scientific knowledge within the system of methods. Its overall process consists of either the extraction of the general and elimination of the particular or the extraction of the particular and neglect of the general. Subjects of abstraction are concepts, attitudes, judgements, and conclusions, etc.

e) Proving is one of the most important scientific methods in which almost all the methods and all the special methodical procedures are incorporated, including: analysis and synthesis, generalization and specialization, induction and deduction, abstraction and concretization, as well as others. The opposite procedure in relation to the process of proving is refuting.

f) The method of compilation is the process of utilizing other people's scientific research results, that is, other people's perceptions, attitudes, conclusions and insights. The comparative method is the comparison process of the same or related phenomena so as to determine the similarities in behaviour and intensity, as well as the differences that exist between them. We should distinguish the total, complete identicalness of all the factors of a whole from the partial identicalness that relates only to certain parts, factors, properties, relationships, changes, etc. We often encounter similar forms whose contents and essence are completely opposite. By applying the comparative method, one can easily discover the specifics, that is, both the advantages and disadvantages of various social phenomena (e.g. modes of production and distribution). The difference between individual economic systems is reflected in the application of different methods in solving the above-mentioned general and similar problems, and the comparative analysis provides significant assistance in this matter. It is worth noting that in most research in the social sciences both methods (inductive and deductive) are used when drawing conclusions.

Special methods

Special methods include: positivism, historical method (method of understanding) and dialectic method.

Positivism

Positivism is the oldest and the most influential methodological approach. In the literature, we can often find the division of positivism into early positivism, neo-positivism and post-positivism. In the broadest sense, positivism represents the rejection of metaphysics. In other words, the term scientific includes only those phenomena that can be seen and measured. According to the positivist worldview, science should help us understand the world well enough as to be able to perform predictions.

Many of our stereotypes about science originate from the period in which that particular direction of philosophy (i.e. positivism) dominated. However, science has progressed in the era of post-positivism, wherein we have overcome many of these stereotypes. Auguste Comte was the founder of early positivism in the second half of the nineteenth century. The most important social sciences (economics, sociology and history) were formed at the time of positivism. Comte advocated the development of the social sciences modelled upon the natural sciences and for their separation from the religious way of thinking. It is for these reasons that positivism has persisted for such a long time, up until the present day.

As it developed, early positivism evolved into neo-positivism (Lazarsfeld). It adhered to all the principles of positivism in addition to introducing a system of measurement in the social sciences, thus advancing the social sciences towards the ideal of the natural sciences. Positivism indicates that only 'factual' knowledge gained through observation, including measurement, is reliable. In fact, positivism relies upon empiricism (based on the idea that observation and measurement is the core of scientific endeavour). According to this opinion, every notion that cannot be translated into the language of variables is unacceptable for modern social sciences.

This principle was brought into question for the first time in the second half of the last century. In fact, many things have changed our views of science since the mid-twentieth century. One of the most accepted forms of post-positivism in philosophy is known as critical realism. Supporters of this direction of thinking believe that we cannot comprehend our reality with absolute certainty based on observation, and therefore all theories are subject to subsequent correction. Based on the results of our research, we can determine whether our theory corresponds to the obtained results. If it does not correspond well, then we have to revise the theory so as to predict reality better. Theories that pass all the tests and measurements and persist are often compared with the natural species that have survived throughout evolution. According to the principles of positivism, knowledge is derived from human experience. Crowther and Lancaster (2008) emphasize the adoption of the deductive approach as a general rule in positivism. Positivism is one of the most suitable approaches for studying the nature of the relationships between phenomena. It has found greater application in business studies than in other disciplines. This is because business relations are made from the integration of relationships among individuals within and among companies.

The principles of positivism are:

a) avoiding subjectivity in the research procedure as much as possible;
b) applying the same principles for the development of natural and social sciences;
c) solving practical problems in society;
d) separating 'normal' from 'pathological' social phenomena – everything that 'stands out' from the average is 'pathological'.

Historical method (method of understanding)

'Subjects of study in qualitative research must be considered from a developmental point of view and comprehensively in their historical dimension taking into account that every current situation or problem is the reflection of some past events' (Primorac, 2010, p. 29). Wilhelm Dilthey founded the method of understanding in the nineteenth century. He made a clear distinction between the natural and the social sciences, believing that all social phenomena and processes have their historical component. In other words, many social phenomena can only be studied scientifically when viewed in their historical context.

Methodology based on the dialectics

Dialectics is the qualitative research method. This method is based on the understanding that all phenomena in nature and in human society are in universal mutual connection. The methodology based on dialectics implies, under the scientific method, a dialectical unity of:

a) logical principles and rules;
b) theoretical knowledge of reality; and
c) practical actions and technical resources that are used in research activities.

General scientific methods

The modern way of acquiring scientific knowledge involves the synthesis of quantitative and qualitative analysis. The quantification of the social sciences is not new. It was introduced in the 1920s, when sociology and economics were young sciences. In this way, their quantification was supposed to strengthen the status of these sciences (McCloskey, 2005). A few decades later, Paul Samuelson (1947) and Kenneth Arrow (1951), in particular, advocated the application of mathematics in economic research.

The genesis of the development and application of mathematical economics, based on logical and other methods, has its roots in the work of the French scientist Cournot (1960). The complementarity of theoretical and empirical research can also be found in the works of Kuznets (1966), Goldsmith (2000), Friedman (1953) and others. In recent times, there are many supporters of the mathematization of economics. For example, Edesess (2012) provides a mathematical approach to some of the key problems facing the economic theory, thus initiating a series of economic debates. The scientist McCloskey (2005) also supported the idea of the mathematization of economics. He believes that the usual objections related to the application of mathematical and statistical methods in economics are unacceptable. In his opinion, the supporters of this view are those scholars who emphasize the superiority of the natural sciences in relation to the social sciences (McCloskey, 2002). Furthermore, the famous French economist Walras once pointed out that 'many economists who do not know mathematics, appear as the biggest critics of its application in solving economic principles' (Walras, 2010). There is also an opinion among economists that it is rather difficult to use mathematics in economics, and hence they advocate that it is better to use some other methods that are not essentially mathematical in nature. However, Edesess (2012) argues that it is not the pervasive use of mathematics in economics that is the source of all the problems and general confusion, but the fact that we should not apply the mathematical model everywhere; that is, the use of the mathematical model is meaningless when something cannot be measured. In his opinion, mathematics is excessively used in economics, and too much of it is considered of poor quality. This mathematical haughtiness is the core of the critical state of economic theory, which was worsened by the financial crisis (Edesess, 2012). In other words, the economy cannot over-rely on accurate mathematical models, considering that we cannot put an equal sign between economics and mathematics.

Box 4.1 The benefits of mathematics in economic analysis

Whether we choose the mathematical or theoretical approach to economic analysis is of little significance, in comparison to the importance of the benefits of mathematics in terms of improving analysis and a higher degree of explicitness on every level of reasoning.

Moreover, mathematical economics should be seen as a special approach to economic analysis, which is fundamentally no different from the non-mathematical. The main distinction between 'mathematical economics' and 'theoretical economics' is reflected in the fact that, within mathematical economics, the assumptions and conclusions are expressed in mathematical symbols instead of words. In addition, the 'language' used in mathematical economics is characterized by conciseness and greater precision, which is not always the case in theoretical economics (Radović, 1996, p. 154).

Finally, it can be concluded that although the quantification of social and economic phenomena has had more opponents than supporters from the very beginning of its application, mathematical-methodological knowledge has passed the test of time and it has not lost its relevance up to the present day.

Points for discussion

1 Explain the basic function of methodology.
2 Discuss what makes up scientific knowledge.
3 Analyse why it is often impossible to study social problems by using experimental methods.
4 Explain the advantages of an interdisciplinary approach to research in the social sciences.

References

Arrow, K. (1951). *Social Choice and Individual Values*. New York: John Wiley & Sons.
Beckert, J. (2013). Capitalism as a system of expectations: Toward a sociological micro-foundation of political economy. *Politics and Society*, 41(3), 323–350.
Bhattacherjee, A. (2012). *Social Science Research: Principles, Methods, and Practices* (2nd edition). Florida: Creative Commons Attribution.
Blaug, M. (1980). *The Methodology of Economics: Or How Economists Explain.* Cambridge: Cambridge University Press.
Cournot, Antoine Augustin (1960) [1838]. *Researches into the Mathematical Principles of the Theory of Wealth*. New York: Kelley.
Crowther, D. and Lancaster, G. (2008). *Research Methods: A Concise Introduction to Research in Management and Business Consultancy*. Oxford: Butterworth-Heinemann.
Edesess, M. (2012). An attack on Paul Krugman. *Advisor Perspectives*. Available at: http://www.advisorperspectives.com/newsletters12/20-krugman2.php
Friedman, M. (1953). The methodology of positive economics. In: *The Methodology of Positive Economics*. Chicago: University of Chicago Press, pp. 3–43.
Goldsmith, E. (2000). Is science neutral? *The Ecologist*, 30(3), 20–23.
Hempel, C. G. and Oppenheim, P. (1948). Studies in the logic of explanation. *Philosophy of Science.* Reprinted (with a postscript) in C. G. Hempel, *Aspects of Scientific Explanation.* New York: Free Press, 1965, pp. 245–295.
Ioannides, S. and Nielsen, K. (2007). *Economics and the Social Sciences: Boundaries, Interaction and Integration*. Cheltenham: Edward Elgar Publishing.
Kulenović, Z. (2005). Metodologija istraživackog rada [Scientific Research Methodology], Faculty of Maritime Studies, University of Split.
Kuznets, S. (1966). *Modern Economic Growth*. New Haven, CT: Yale University Press.

McCloskey, D. (2002). *The Secret Sins of Economics*. Chicago: Prickly Paradigm Press.

McCloskey, D. (2005). *History of Economic Ideas*, XIII(3), 85–102.

Martin, R. (2011). The limits of the scientific method in economics and the world. Available at: http://blogs.reuters.com/great-debate/2011/11/11/the-limits-of-the-scientific-method-in-economics-and-the-world/

Ostle, B. and Mensing, R. (1975). *Statistics in Research* (3rd edition). Ames, IA: Iowa State University Press.

Poli, R. (2014). Anticipation: A new thread for the human and social sciences? *Cadmus*, 2(3), 22–49.

Primorac, Z. (2010). Uvod u filozofiju znanosti [Introduction to the Philosophy of Science], University of Mostar.

Radović, M. (1996). Ekonomska analiza na novim (kvantitativnim) osnovama [Economic analysis on new (quantitative basis)]. In: R. Aničić (Ed.) *Uvod u metode ekonomske analize-teorijsko filozofske osnove naučnog metoda* [*Introduction to the Method of Economic Analysis and Theoretical Philosophical Underpinnings of the Scientific Method*]. Faculty of Economics, University of Belgrade.

Robinson, J. (1962). *Economic Philosophy*. London: Watts.

Samuelson, P. A. (1947). *Foundations of Economic Analysis*. Cambridge, MA: Harvard University Press.

Walras, L. (2010). *Elements of Pure Economics*. London: Routledge Library Editions: Economics.

5 Design and implementation strategy of qualitative methods in scientific research

Conducting qualitative and quantitative research not only involves different methods for collecting and analyzing data, but also the use of various research strategies. The most important differences between these studies are based on different strategies.

(Witt, 2001)

Qualitative methods: introductory considerations

The relationship between academic theory and practice in the social sciences changed dramatically in the final decade of the last century. The extensive reading on qualitative research, which foregrounds this type of research and considers it only in an academic context, has greatly contributed to this (Denzin and Lincoln, 2000).

From the end of the nineteenth and during the twentieth century, qualitative research methods evolved and became widely adopted. Their usefulness meant that they quickly found a place in almost all scientific disciplines, including those that traditionally used controlled experiments in the study of human behaviour. Particularly at the end of the twentieth century, qualitative research became popular and widely applied in market research (Walker, 1985), psychological research (Richardson, 1996), and sociology and other social sciences (Gilhooly and Green, 1996). As the application of qualitative methods spread, the number of approaches and modalities of their implementation also grew. Multiple applications of different techniques and methods made it difficult for researchers to agree on a single definition of qualitative research. Nelson *et al.* (1992) was among the first who attempted to offer a comprehensive definition, describing qualitative research as an 'interdisciplinary, transdisciplinary, and sometimes contra disciplinary field' (p. 4).

Qualitative research aims at comprehending a problem that is being studied from the perspective of a local population. This type of research is particularly useful for getting specific information about the beliefs, opinions, behaviour and social context of individual populations. Qualitative methods are also useful for the recognition of intangible factors, such as social norms, socio-economic status, gender roles and others, whose place in research may not be so obvious. When combined with quantitative research, they can contribute to a better interpretation of a complex social phenomenon that represents the subject of research. Thus, the 'qualitative approach implements a wide range of unrelated methods, with the aim of always providing better results or improving the existing one for a phenomenon that is being observed and analyzed' (Denzin and Lincoln, 2000, p. 2).

Characteristics of qualitative approaches

In defining the characteristics of qualitative research, some researchers have focused their attention on key aspects of the methodology (Bryman, 1988; Denzin and Lincoln, 2000; Hammersley and Atkinson, 1995; Holloway and Wheeler, 1996; Mason, 2002; Miles and Huberman, 1994; Patton, 2002).

Key aspects include the overall perspective of research; the flexibility of research; the scope and quality of qualitative data; the unique approach to the analysis and interpretation of data; and the types of results stemming from qualitative research.

Qualitative research studies social phenomena in their natural setting. Furthermore, qualitative research involves the collection and selection of empirical material founded on the analysis of textual materials that are created based on personal experiences, individual and group interviews, observations and other types of records on the studied phenomena.

It is important to recognize that there is no generally accepted way of conducting qualitative research. The way in which a particular scientific research is conducted depends on many factors:

a)   research objectives and tasks;
b)   knowledge and skills of researchers;
c)   characteristics of research participants;
d)   financial resources;
e)   conditions of research.

Qualitative research strives at providing answers to the following questions:

a)   Why do people behave the way they do?
b)   How are opinions and viewpoints formed?
c)   In what way are the external events affecting people?

Parker expands the framework of qualitative research, which is determined by: (a) an attempt to capture the sense that lies within what we are saying, and which structures what we do; (b) an elaboration and systematization of the significance of an identified phenomenon; (c) an attempt to understand and explain other people's interpretations of the meaning of a particular issue or problem (Parker, 1999). Moreover, the 'qualitative research always studies subjects in their historical and social context, trying to understand and interpret the meaning or significance of their activities, practice and everyday experience' (Ševkušić, 2006, p. 305).

The objectives of qualitative analysis

The objectives of qualitative analysis involve a more complete and deeper understanding of research phenomena. This is achieved through:

a) exhaustive study of other people' experiences who find themselves in close or more frequent contact with the studied phenomenon, thus considering their perceptions of a phenomenon (competent interlocutors);
b) organized observation of a particular phenomenon if this phenomenon is available;
c) study of material evidences related to the phenomenon that represents the subject of our research.

Similarities and differences between qualitative and quantitative methods

Qualitative methods encourage uninhibited and creative thinking about a problem. These methods are far more graphic and more meaningful when it is necessary to achieve a deeper and fuller understanding of a particular social phenomenon. They are characterized by flexibility and sensitivity to the social context in which the data are collected. Moreover, they also provide greater freedom in shaping cognitive processes.

Qualitative research differs from quantitative research in five key aspects (Primorac, 2010):

a) use of positivist and post-positivist methodology;
b) acceptance of postmodern sensibility;
c) study of a particular subject from its perspective within its historical, social and cultural context;
d) study of the world of everyday life;
e) rich descriptions that are provided by qualitative researchers.

The key difference between quantitative and qualitative methods is their flexibility. Qualitative methods are usually more flexible – that is, they allow for greater spontaneity and interaction between researchers and participants in the study. For example, qualitative methods generally use 'open' questions. In addition, the relationship between researchers and study participants in qualitative methods is often less formal than in quantitative research.

Moreover, quantitative and qualitative research methods differ in:

a) their analytical objectives;
b) types of questions that arise;
c) types of instruments used in collecting data, etc.

In addition to these differences, there are also differences in the philosophical roots of qualitative and quantitative methods. Primorac (2010) makes a clear distinction between the two of them in this regard, linking quantitative methods to

English analytical philosophy and the logical positivism of the Vienna Circle, while stressing the origin of qualitative research methods in the German School.

When should we choose the qualitative research method?

Reasons for choosing the qualitative approach may include the following (see also Table 5.1):

a)   the nature of a research question (e.g. understanding organizational behaviour in a company, employee motivation, and similar issues);
b)   insufficient knowledge about a particular phenomenon (e.g. key factors in the selection process of strategies that should contribute to the recovery of the selected organization);
c)   deepening knowledge about a familiar phenomenon (e.g. what do the employees think about the reward system in a particular organization?);
d)   clarification of quantitative findings;
e)   directing the practical work of experts;
f)   generating findings for commercial use;
g)   creating new (thorough) knowledge.

There are opposing opinions among researchers regarding the quality of research methods and the scope of their application. Quantativists consider qualitative researchers 'soft' scientists or parascientists, as they use methods and techniques that do not possess the power of evidence as in the natural sciences (Primorac, 2010). 'They usually criticize the supporters of quantitative research due to the insufficient connection between propositional and experiential knowledge' (Ševkušić, 2006, p. 313). Therefore, the number of supporters for the application of mixed methods in economics and other research within the social sciences is growing.

The synthesis of the qualitative and quantitative approaches to the study of social phenomena: the mixed methods

During the last decade, there has been a small explosion in the use of quantitative approaches in research, including the 'mixed methods' that apply a combination of qualitative and quantitative methods. The usefulness of mixed methods is

Table 5.1 Reasons for choosing the qualitative approach

To study complex phenomena that are difficult to measure quantitatively
To follow organizational processes and their changes over time; describe social interactions
To generate the necessary data for a complete understanding of a problem
To provide detailed descriptions of the individual perceptions and experiences

Source: Retrieved from: http://circ.ahajournals.org/content/119/10/1442/T1.

increasingly apparent, given that they are using the advantages of the different aspects of both qualitative and quantitative research. For example, a preliminary qualitative component can be used in order to generate hypotheses or form the contents of a questionnaire that will be used in the subsequent quantitative study. Strategies for improving the validity of mixed methods imply respecting the methodological assumptions of each approach within research. Mixed (quantitative and qualitative) methods of research provide the opportunities to integrate different theoretical perspectives (e.g. environmental, economic, sociological and other theories). These methods are used when quantitative or qualitative approaches are not sufficient by themselves to study a problem from multiple perspectives and thus fully understand it. The main objective of mixed research methods is to analyse a phenomenon, a problem or a question from any of the relevant angles, using, where appropriate, previous research and/or more than one type of research technique. Another term for mixed methods can also be found in the literature: that is, multiple methodology. These methods offer the best of both approaches within a research project, which is reflected in an in-depth analysis. A review of the literature suggests that a large number of economic studies are done using qualitative and mixed methods, with an emphasis on the benefits of their use. Despite the fact that qualitative methods are often considered less reliable, less precise than quantitative methods, combining quantitative with qualitative approaches has its advantages; that is, their usefulness depends on the specific questions that represent the subject of study.

There are many ways in which qualitative and quantitative data analysis can be combined. However, the decision as to what extent a particular phenomenon is to be observed through quantitative or qualitative methods in research depends on several things:

a) the preferred philosophical approach;
b) the skills and abilities to use methods for data collection and analysis;
c) topic and subject of the research.

Box 5.1 Usefulness of mixed methods

Example:

We were initially interested in an analysis that was primarily quantitative, looking at social trends or political implications. However, we also wanted to conduct several interviews to ask individuals how they perceive particular events. Data obtained in both ways will give us a clearer and better picture of the phenomenon that is being studied, which is the aim of using mixed methods.

Design of mixed research methods

There is no rigid formula for the design of mixed research methods, but the following general guidelines should be followed:

a) it is necessary to do preliminary considerations;
b) think about the theoretical and philosophical settings of a problem;
c) think about the reasons for using mixed methods;
d) analyse how the quantitative and qualitative methods can be integrated into the research process.

Draft of qualitative research

In addition to a procedural framework, the draft of a research project leads us towards specific research strategies that are available within the qualitative methodology (Primorac, 2010).

The draft should include:

a) the preliminary definition of a particular topic and research problems;
b) possible research objectives;
c) the significance and justification of the research;
d) basic hypothetical opinions about the problem;
e) the definition of key terms;
f) basic methods and techniques;
g) conducting research and collecting relevant data;
h) writing reports on conducted research.

The entire research process should be under constant supervision, which implies continual and rigorous methodical control of all phases. The researcher must explicate and explain the individual steps in the procedures so that other independent observers can easily verify them (Primorac, 2010).

The selection and formulation of questions in qualitative research

This is the most creative part of the research and is essential for future work. Why was the specific topic chosen?

a) Because of its actuality or attractiveness?
b) Because of the requirements of practice or professional scientific interest?
c) As a result of possessing knowledge and experience?
d) Because of the disposition of empirical data?

Setting research objectives

Research objectives should be clearly defined, and directed towards the problem that is being treated. Is it possible to set several objectives?

Defining basic concepts

In research, it is necessary to precisely define phenomena that represent the subject of consideration. An initiation of research without clear definitions can cause a lot of confusion. Therefore, the researchers are required to:

a) state the main approaches used to determine basic concepts;
b) indicate their orientation, or give their own definition, which differs from the existing ones;
c) explain their choice.

Writing the research proposal

The proposal is the argument for the realization of research. The research proposal should be written clearly and concisely. It should demonstrate that the study has:

a) an original approach;
b) an exact description of the method;
c) a specification of objectives.

Forming hypotheses

The hypothesis indicates the assumption of a researcher about the solution of a chosen problem. It relies upon the known and generates the cognition of the unknown. The first step in forming a hypothesis requires collecting as many observations as possible on the problem that is being explored. Furthermore, it is necessary to select among them and to extract only those observations that could

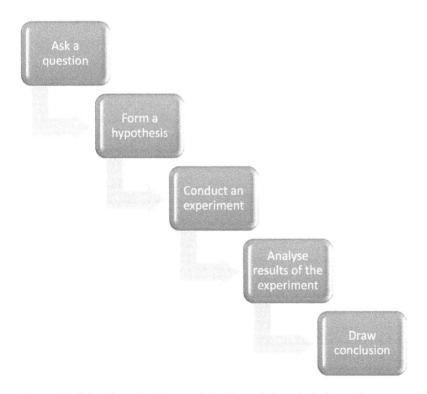

Figure 5.1 Scientific method (source: https://www.help.optimizely.com/)

be directly related to the problem. The assumptions of possible explanations for the causes of the problem are then given, and finally the assessment of explanations that can be tested as hypotheses.

The hypothesis must be precisely set, so that it can be more easily verifiable (i.e. tested). There should be at least three hypotheses that should be studied individually, and their accuracy determined.

Basic concepts in the context of testing hypotheses

In the context of statistical analysis, we often talk about the null hypothesis and the alternative hypothesis. If we compare the advantages of method A with method B, under the assumption that both methods are equally good, we call this assumption the null hypothesis. In contrast, if we assume that method A is superior to method B, then we can call this assumption the alternative hypothesis. The null hypothesis is usually denoted as H0 and the alternative hypothesis as Ha.

EXAMPLE

Let us suppose that we want to test the hypothesis that the mean value of the population (m) is equal to the assumed mean value of the population (mH0) = 100. Then, we could say that the mean value of the population is equal to the hypothetical mean value of 100, which can be expressed as:

$$H0: m = mH0 = 0\ 100$$

If our results do not support this null hypothesis, we can then conclude that something else is true. The rejection of the null hypothesis is known as the alternative hypothesis. In other words, a group of alternatives to the null hypothesis are alternative hypotheses. If we have accepted hypothesis H0, then we have rejected Ha; if we have accepted hypothesis Ha, then we have rejected H0. In most cases, the final decision whether to accept or reject the null hypothesis is based on the use of an appropriate statistical test. Certain statistical software, such as SPSS, automatically calculates the likelihood of the obtained result of a statistical test.

When the null hypothesis is formulated, we should usually take into account the following:

a)   The null hypothesis is the hypothesis that we are trying to reject, while the alternative hypothesis represents all other possibilities. Namely, the null hypothesis is exclusively tested and the alternative hypothesis is accepted or rejected indirectly.
b)   The research always starts from the assumption that the null hypothesis is true and that the 'difference' is not statistically significant.
c)   The accuracy of the null hypothesis is determined through specific significance tests. Fixed probability for false rejection of the null hypothesis H0 is marked with the Greek letter α. In the social sciences, the level of significance is usually $\alpha = 0.05$, that is, 5 per cent.

Preliminary research (pilot research)

> The researcher usually plans a one-time research, which begins with the exploration (getting to know a phenomenon), its description (precise description and definition of it), and ends with the explication (explanation) and prediction (prediction of other phenomena based on it).
>
> (Lalović, 2014, p. 14)

Preliminary research is performed on a sample of 5-10 per cent of the sample size that is planned for the final research, and has the function of (a) verifying the research instruments and (b) evaluating the organization of research.

Conclusion

Whether we are planning our own research projects, or studying someone else's research results, a good knowledge of methods and making the proper choices has many advantages. This knowledge contributes to a greater confidence in our own opinions, as well as improving the capacity for an evaluation of the opinions of others. In addition, a good knowledge of methods may have an impact on the motivation of researchers to examine their own knowledge on various issues.

Given that research still has some limitations and shortcomings, our results will always be open to different interpretations. However, even in the areas of research that are full of controversy, the search for new and more sophisticated research has value.

Points for discussion

1 Explain when we should use qualitative research in social sciences.
2 What are the advantages and disadvantages of qualitative methods?
3 Analyse and explain mixed methods.

References

Bryman, A. (1988). *Quantity and Quality in Social Research.* London: Unwin Hyman.

Denzin, N. K. and Lincoln, Y. S. (Eds) (2000). *The Handbook of Qualitative Research.* London: Sage.

Gilhooly, K. and Green, C. (1996). Protocol analysis: theoretical background. In: J. Richardson (Ed.). *Handbook of Qualitative Research Methods for Psychology and the Social Sciences.* Leicester: BPS Books, pp. 43–54.

Hammersley, M. and Atkinson, P. (1995). *Ethnography: Principles in Practice* (2nd edition). London: Routledge.

Holloway, I. and Wheeler, S. (1996). *Qualitative Research for Nurses.* Oxford: Blackwell Science.

Lalović, Z. (2014). Metodologija naučno-istraživačkog rada sa osnovama statistike [Methodology of scientific research with the basics of statistics]. Available at: http://bs.scribd.com/doc/200326625/Metodologija-naucnog-istrazivanja#scribd

Mason, J. (2002). *Qualitative Researching* (2nd edition). London: Sage.

Miles, M. and Huberman, M. (1994). *Qualitative Data Analysis: An Expanded Sourcebook.* Thousand Oaks, CA: Sage.

Nelson, C., Treichler, P. and Grossberg, L. (1992). Cultural studies. In: L. Grossberg, C. Nelson and P. Treichler (Eds). *Cultural Studies.* New York: Routledge, pp. 1–16.

Parker, I. (Ed.) (1999). *Deconstructing Psychotherapy.* London: Sage.

Patton, M. Q. (2002). *Qualitative Research and Evaluation Methods* (3rd edition). Thousand Oaks, CA: Sage.

Primorac, Z. (2010). Uvod u filozofiju znanosti. [Introduction to the philosophy of science]. University of Mostar.

Radović-Marković, M. (2013). Various communication modalities in organizations with focus on virtual firms. In: K. Larsen, G. Vzov, K. Krumov and J. Schneider (Eds). *Advances in International Psychology: Research Approaches and Personal Dispositions, Socialization Processes and Organizational Behavior.* Kassel, Germany: Kassel University Press / Sofia, Bulgaria: VUZF University.

Richardson, J. (1996). *Handbook of Qualitative Research Methods for Psychology and the Social Sciences.* Oxford: Wiley-Blackwell.

Ševkušić, S. (2006). Osnovne metodološke postavke kvalitativnih istraživanja [Basic methodological assumptions of qualitative research]. *Zbornik instituta za pedagoška istraživanja* [*Journal of the Institute for Educational Research*], 38(2), 299–316.

Walker, R. (Ed.) (1985). *Applied Qualitative Research.* Aldershot: Gower.

Witt, H. (2001). Strategies in qualitative and quantitative research. *Qualitative and Quantitative Research: Conjunctions and Divergences*, 2(1) (2001).

6   Methods and techniques of data collection

The choice of research techniques depends on the available data.

(Russell, 1962, p. 1)

Qualitative techniques

Qualitative researchers should use methods of analysis that are explicit and systematic (Greenhalgh and Taylor, 1997). Some experts argue that it is sufficient for only one researcher to perform data collection and analysis (Gubrium, 2007; Malterud, 2001). In these cases, the awareness and the attention of researchers in order to avoid potential bias is very important. Other experts suggest that the quality and comprehensiveness of the analysis are improved if the research involves more researchers from different scientific disciplines (Patton, 1999; Pope *et al.*, 2000).

A multidisciplinary analytical team can generate unique insights into a particular problem from different perspectives, participate in critical discussions on vague data, and ensure thorough consideration and interpretation of the data. In either approach, the scientists have to seek and examine negative cases and provide possible explanations as to why the data differ (Mays and Pope, 1995).

There are a number of specific techniques that use qualitative and mixed methods (Crabtree and Miller, 1999; Creswell and Plano Clark, 2007), in order to enhance the credibility and reliability of qualitative research.

When used properly, qualitative techniques seek answers to questions by examining various social phenomena. Certain authors associate qualitative research with only one technique, that is, with direct observation of a phenomenon. However, most scientists also add other types of techniques to this technique.

The analysis of qualitative data, collected by means of some of the techniques, allows the researchers to scrutinize various social phenomena and use them to create social reality. They will all be considered here.

Characteristics and types of techniques

A good technique should ensure measures that are:

a)   reliable: so that the results obtained through the measurement can be relied on;
b)   stable: that is, not dependent on the measurement time or the person making the measurement;
c)   valid: that is, actually measure what they are supposed to measure (i.e. to construct what needs to be explored).

There are three basic types of techniques:

a)   direct observation;
b)   verbal techniques (interview and questionnaire);
c)   analysis of contents.

How do we choose a technique?

We choose a particular research technique depending on the research question. Different techniques provide different types of information. Combining techniques gives results that are more reliable.

The method of direct observation

One of the earliest and most widely used methods in science in general, observation is one of the methods of scientific data collection, using direct sensory perception of the manifestations of a particular phenomenon. Observation is a qualitative research method of behaviour, events and processes, through which the subject of research is systematically and precisely monitored and described. This technique involves the direct observation of phenomena in their natural setting. Observational research (or field research) is a kind of correlational (i.e. non-experimental) research. There are various types of research based on this method; each of them has both advantages and disadvantages.

Observation can be divided by subject into:

a)   observation of events;
b)   observation of processes;
c)   observation of social phenomena.

This method of research differs from experimental research, which is conducted in controlled laboratory conditions. It is irreplaceable when it comes to processes, behaviours and events that can only take place and be followed in authentic 'natural conditions' (i.e. those that can be neither artificially caused nor simulated).

This research method is particularly widespread in the social sciences and in marketing. For example, case studies are a special kind of research based on the method of observation. However, its typical limitations consist in the inability to explore the actual causes of behaviours.

Techniques based on verbal communication

The techniques that are based on verbal communication can be divided into:

a) oral communication: an interview (unstructured, semi-structured, structured);
b) written communication: a questionnaire.

Box 6.1 Pros and cons of techniques of verbal communication

Key advantages:

- We can examine the phenomena that are not available through external observation.
- It is possible to obtain data and information faster, cheaper and easier.

Key disadvantages:

- Respondents are always aware that they are examined.
- There are many opportunities for them to change their answers under the influence of various factors.

The interview

The interview represents the gathering of data through verbal communication between the interviewer and the interviewee; the content is determined by the purpose of the scientific research. Interviews are conducted by trained interviewers, using the same protocol as in surveys; that is, a standardized set of questions. Unlike the questionnaire, the interview may contain special instructions for the interviewer, and may include the space for conversation and the recording of special observations and comments. In addition, the interviewer has the opportunity to clarify any issues raised by the respondent. However, the conversations are time-consuming and very demanding.

The most typical form of interview is a conversation with the individual or 'face to face' interview, where the interviewer directly asks the questions and records the answers of the respondent. Depending on the scientific objective, interviews can be free or undirected, directed, or in-depth and panel interviews.

a) Free interview: This is used to collect general data on the phenomenon that is being examined. Great freedom is allowed in asking questions.
b) Directive or in-depth interview: This is used to collect data on the deep, hidden layers of the particular phenomenon that is being examined. They allow minimum freedom to the researchers.
c) Panel interview: This represents a specific type of directed interview which is used to study long-term and changing social phenomena. It is performed at certain intervals; the essential criteria for distinguishing interviews from surveys are different procedures of examination.

Focus groups

Focus groups include group interviews organized on a specific subject and on a particular segment of the population, in order to collect data of interest to the researchers. The focus group is a small group of respondents (usually 6–10 respondents), who are collectively questioned at the same place. The special advantage of a focus group relates to the fact that it enables dialogue between participants.

Focus groups are used for the detailed examination of complex issues. They are considered particularly useful in market research. They are also convenient for pilot studies, which form part of the research project.

Role of the interviewer

The interviewer has a complex role in the interview process, which includes the following tasks:

a) Prepare for the interview: The success of completed work depends largely on the preparation of the interviewer. Therefore, the interviewer must be well trained in the interview process.
b) Establish cooperation with the respondent.
c) Motivate respondents: The motivation of respondents depends largely on the interviewer. If the interviewer is disinterested or inattentive, respondents will not be motivated to provide useful answers.
d) Clarify any inaccuracies or problems: Interviewers must be able to quickly solve unforeseen problems as soon as they arise.

The (questionnaire) survey

The survey is an investigating technique in which there is no direct, personal communication between examiners and examinees, as the test is done through a written questionnaire. The questionnaire is delivered to the respondents, who are selected based on a particular sample, and they are asked to respond to questions in accordance with instructions from the questionnaire. Although census surveys were conducted in ancient Egypt, it was only in the 1930/40s that they began to be used as a formal research method, thanks to the sociologist Lazarsfeld. This method has since become a very popular method for research in the social sciences.

The survey is best suited for studies that are focused on the individual as the unit of analysis (Bhattacherjee, 2012). It has several important advantages over other methods of research. According to Leary (1995), there are distinct advantages in using questionnaires in comparison to interviews: questionnaires are cheaper and easier to use, and they provide confidentiality and security in obtaining data. In addition, surveys are an excellent means for measuring a wide range of data, such as the characteristics of respondents (e.g. the motivation in

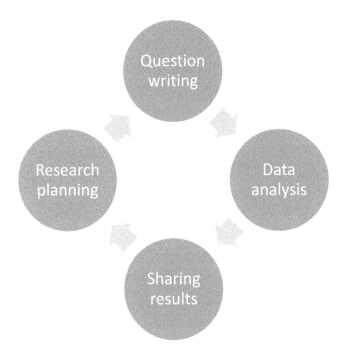

Figure 6.1 The key steps in the survey process

the workplace – Figure 6.1), attitudes (e.g. towards their managers), opinions (e.g. on new rules of procedure), behaviour (e.g. open communication with the bosses), or factual information (e.g. monthly salary). In addition, the survey is ideal for collecting data remotely with the help of e-mail and online surveys, as well as over the phone. It should be noted that this type of research is cost-effective in terms of saving time for the researchers, as well as effort and cost, compared with most other methods.

The survey process

Surveys are the most common techniques used for collecting socio-economic data from individuals. The process of drafting and implementing the survey is relatively simple. However, the data collected through surveys can be of little or no use if they are not well designed and implemented.

Types of surveys: the online survey

The online survey consists of one or a small number of questions (Figure 6.2). It is placed on the Internet, or on the website next to other content. The goal is to examine the opinion of the respondents in a relatively short period of time.

*Required
Name
[ ]

Email address
[ ]

Country*
[ ]

Gender *
[▼]

Age *
[▼]

Education*
[▼]

How many years have you been working for your current employer?*
[▼]

It is important that the institution I work for offers me "job promotion" *
[▼]

I would work harder if I know that they will compensate it with a higher salary*
[▼]

It is important to have an interesting job*
[▼]

I would leave my job if I do not enjoy it*
[▼]

What is the most important motivating factor for you?*
[▼]

Do you feel empowered in your organization?*
[▼]

Is there any kind of "gender discrimination" in your organization?*
[▼]

Is there any kind of "age discrimination" in your institution?*
[▼]

Does your organization offer the employees an opportunity to participate in decision making?*
[▼]

Figure 6.2 Online survey – employee motivation (source: Radović-Marković, 2013)

The elements of good online surveys are:

a) pay special attention to the first question: the first question is the largest generator of respondents' withdrawal;
b) the format of questions should be similar to the format of a hard copy questionnaire;
c) adjust the length and format of each question;
d) attach the appropriate instructions along with the question;
e) prevent the possibility of respondents skipping questions;
f) be careful with questions with many possible answers, etc.

Types of surveys: mail surveys

These can be used to collect large amounts of information at a very low cost per respondent. Robson (1993) emphasized, in addition to the low cost, that mail surveys are extremely effective for obtaining information in a relatively short period of time. Also, the interviewer has no influence on the respondents' answers. One other benefit is that it offers respondents the possibility of answering questions when they have enough time.

The formulation of questions

Questions should be clear, understandable, simple, and given in a logical order. They should also be reduced to only the necessary number. Furthermore, it is advisable to avoid suggestive and ambiguous questions. The order in which questions are presented should be taken into account as well. Sensitive questions, such as questions about income, and the consumption of alcohol or drugs, should be placed at the end of the survey. This contributes to creating trust among respondents, so that they can respond to questions more easily and with less delay.

Box 6.2 Formulation of questions

Example

1   How often do you buy domestic products?
2   Do you think that domestic products are of high quality?
3   What do you pay attention to when shopping?
4   Do you think that domestic products are of better quality than imported products?
5   Are you going to buy domestic products in the future?

The reason for using open questions is the need to get some unexpected information, which can be used in the study (they are useful for 'sensitive' questions, opinions, attitudes, and things that are not sufficiently known to the researcher). It is good to use them when smaller groups are involved (fewer than 50 respondents). However, in the case of a larger sample, this method of data collection is time-consuming and loaded with errors.

Closed questions

Respondents are offered answers in advance among which they have to choose the most appropriate response. The following guidelines apply:

a)   offered responses should not overlap in meaning;
b)   the respondent chooses an answer from those that are offered;
c)   dichotomous (Yes/No);
d)   multiple choices (never/rarely/often/regularly);
e)   the Likert scale is often used for ranking answers in closed questions; it shows the level of agreement or disagreement with a large number of statements in connection with the attitude or object of observation; individual items are added up and the total score per respondent is obtained.

When are the closed questions advisable? When the researcher is only interested in certain aspects of the problem and does not want to expand information?

Box 6.3 An example of a closed question

Please rate how much you agree or disagree with the following statement: 'I feel good and appreciated at the workplace.'
   The following responses are offered:

a)   I agree entirely.
b)   I partially agree.
c)   I disagree.

The evaluation of usability of a particular questionnaire is made in relation to two criteria: validity and reliability. The validity of a questionnaire indicates the efficiency with which it measures what the researcher wants, while the reliability represents the characteristic of a questionnaire and of the very measurement procedure that enables the consistency of measurement to some extent; that is, it ensures that the same or very similar results are obtained in repeated measurements by means of the same instrument and on the same sample of phenomena.

Data processing and analysis

When the research is completed the data are entered into an already prepared database and then statistically and logically analysed.

The procedures used in qualitative analysis

a)   data reduction;
b)   summarizing existing materials in accordance with the theoretical framework of the research;
c)   extraction of important data and omission of less important data;
d)   coding or data clustering;
e)   display of data;
f)   transparent presentation of summarized findings in a format that allows conclusions to be drawn;
g)   tables, charts or description of the research results are used;
h)   conclusions are drawn;
i)   the conclusions usually take the form of comparing the obtained data that refers to the subject of research.

Analytical strategies

Analysis through the draft

Even the script of an interview or the plan of observation may serve as the backbone of the systematization of collected data.

Although the very plan of research can be changed or supplemented in accordance with new findings, it can still serve as the first provisional organizational scheme.

The interim analysis

The interim analysis is conducted in the course of research in order to focus the researcher's attention on any new aspects that have emerged. It also serves to correct any omissions in the conceptualization of the analysis.

Repeating procedures in a circular analysis

By alternating induction (making assumptions and theoretical explanations based on the synthesis of data) and deduction (testing the theory by means of collected facts), we are conducting a thought simulation of a general way for providing a scientific contribution. Once an assumption is imposed by means of inductive analysis, its verification, which seeks to confirm or refute what was previously concluded, is pending.

Drawing conclusions in qualitative research

Qualitative research draws conclusions and tests them in a special way. Interpretation is based on a large number of procedures called 'tactics of extracting sense'. Therefore, interpretation in qualitative research should stand the test of validity and reliability.

The validity of qualitative research findings

The main tools for interpreting qualitative data are based on logic, in which numbers are replaced with words. The threats to validity are related to the researcher's bias.
There is a potential for many types of errors:

a) the interpretation of events by 'boosting' the data, that is, by using collected data that was obtained from a smaller group of respondents for the entire sample;
b) overvaluation of the data obtained from respondents with a higher level of education and intellectual abilities in relation to those with lower levels;
c) agreeing to adopt viewpoints and offered interpretations of a group that represents the subject of research;
d) the validation methods of the research results.

Quality of data

a) validating the representativeness;
b) validating the influence of researchers;
c) weighting data (some data are more valuable or more credible than others).

Testing explanations

a)   if–then tests;
b)   exclude false connections;
c)   recurrent findings;
d)   results are often given to other researchers for assessment (in many universities, master and doctoral students present the results of their research before they are completed in order to get comments from their colleagues and professors).

Points for discussion

1   Identify the essential difference between the interview and the survey.
2   Why exactly are the focus groups considered particularly useful?
3   Design interview questions for focus groups.
4   Explain at what point the Likert scale is used?

References

Bhattacherjee, A. (2012). *Social Science Research: Principles, Methods, and Practices* (2nd edition). Florida: Creative Commons Attribution.

Crabtree, B. and Miller, W. (Eds) (1999). *Doing Qualitative Research* (2nd edition). Newbury Park, CA: Sage.

Creswell, J. W. and Plano Clark, V. (2007). *Designing and Conducting Mixed Methods Research*. Thousand Oaks, CA: Sage.

Greenhalgh, T. and Taylor, R. (1997). How to read a paper: papers that go beyond numbers (qualitative research). *British Medical Journal*, 315(7110), 740–743.

Gubrium, J. F. (2007). Qualitative methods today. In: L. Curry, R. Shield and T. Wetle (Eds). *Improving Aging and Public Health Research: Qualitative and Mixed Methods*. Washington, DC: American Public Health Association and Gerontological Society of America, pp. 15–25.

Leary, M. (1995). *Behavioural Research Methods*. Pacific Grove, CA: Brooks/Cole.

Malterud, K. (2001). Qualitative research: standards, challenges, and guidelines. *Lancet*, 358, 483–488.

Mays, N. and Pope, C. (1995). Rigour and qualitative research. *British Medical Journal*, 311(6997), 109–112.

Patton, M. Q. (1999). Enhancing the quality and credibility of qualitative analysis. *Health Services Research*, 34(5), 1189–1208.

Pope, C., Ziebland, S. and Mays, N. (2000). Qualitative research in health care: analysing qualitative data. *British Medical Journal*, 320, 114–116.

Robson, C. (1993). *Real World Research. A Resource for Social Scientists and Practitioner-Researchers*. Oxford: Blackwell.

Russell, A. L. (1962). *Scientific Method*. New York: John Wiley & Sons.

Part II

Research paper organization and content

7 Structure of a research paper

A research paper is structured in three major sections: (a) the initial or preliminary sections; (b) the text of the document; and (c) the final section (Figure 7.1). The preliminary section might vary according to the requirements of each institution, but it always includes the first pages of the document. These range from the cover to all the information prior to the actual text of the document. The text is the most important part of the document. The final section includes the references list and appendices (Figure 7.2).

Each part of the document has a specific purpose in the research process. This section will explain each of these sections to clarify its structure.

Preliminary sections

The preliminary sections include the information that precedes the text of the document (Figure 7.3). The structure may vary according to the requirements of each institution; however, it usually includes the following subsections:

a)   Cover
b)   Copyright notice
c)   Committee approval (for doctoral theses)
d)   Executive summary (or abstract)

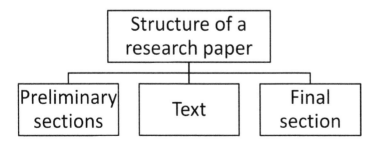

Figure 7.1 The structure of a research paper

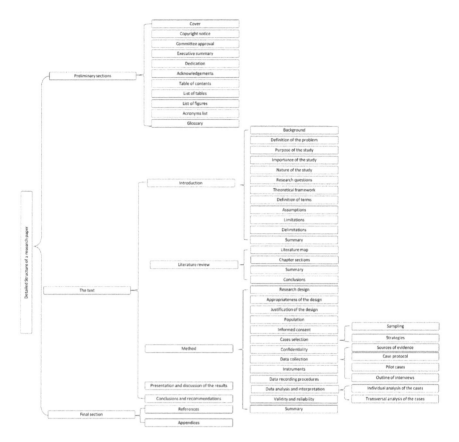

Figure 7.2 Detailed structure of a research paper

e) Dedication
f) Acknowledgements
g) Table of Contents
h) List of tables
i) List of figures
j) Acronyms list (if required)
k) Glossary (if required).

Appendix 7.A shows a complete sample of the preliminary sections retrieved from Avolio's doctoral dissertation (2010). It is important to confirm with the institution to which the research paper is to be submitted the required cover design and the order of the preliminary sections. Some specific recommendations related to the main preliminary sections are presented below.

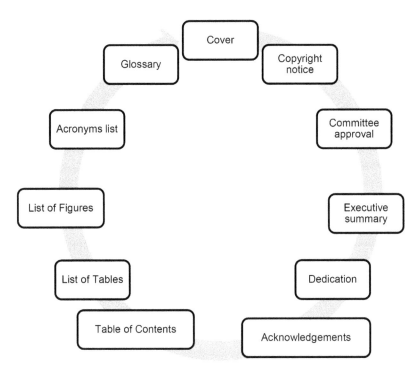

Figure 7.3 Preliminary sections

Executive summary

The executive summary or abstract is a summary of the research content. It provides the interested party with a clear idea of the study without reading the entire document. Although it is included in the preliminary section, it is usually the last thing you write in a research paper.

According to Koopman (1997), the abstract should comprise the following parts (usually, each part must be one sentence long or two parts could merge into one sentence):

a) Motivation: Why are the problem and the results important? This part may include the importance of the research, the difficulty in the field, and the impact of the study.
b) Problem statement: This part explains the problem to be solved and the scope of the situation.
c) Purpose of the study: This part explains how the stated problem will be solved, which variables the study will measure, and the study objectives and hypotheses.

d)   Method: The method applied in the study is explained in detail.
e)   Results: The results are presented clearly and concretely.
f)   Study conclusions.

Some important considerations when writing an abstract are (Koopman, 1997):

a)   It must be understandable, simple, informative, accurate, complete, concise, and specific.
b)   For papers published in scientific journals, it is recommended that the abstract does not to exceed 120 words (American Psychological Association, 2006). In theses and dissertations, it is suggested that is does not exceed 320 words (the standard is 300). In technical reports it should be a minimum of 200 words and a maximum of 350.
c)   It must be written in the third person and in the past tense when referring to the conducted research.
d)   It should not be used only to introduce the topic as that is the purpose of the introduction.
e)   It is not a verbatim copy of the introduction or any other sections; it should stand alone as a completely separate section.
f)   It should not be written as a future plan with phrases such as: 'this paper will attempt to analyse' or 'the paper will look to'. It is a report of what was carried out throughout the research.
g)   Do not to include general and vague phrases such as: 'this abstract will appear'.
h)   Do not include a lot of data without an argument or conclusion. An abstract is a story that is read from beginning to end.
i)   Do not include abbreviations, acronyms or symbols.

For more details on how to write abstracts, refer to Koopman (1997) and Cremmins (1996).

Figure 7.4 depicts an example of an executive summary, based on a dissertation by one of the authors (Avolio, 2010).

Executive Summary

The study identifies the profile of women entrepreneurs in Peru by exploring qualitatively their demographic characteristics; their education, work and family backgrounds; their administrative skills; the nature of their enterprises; the driving factors to become entrepreneurs; and the obstacles for the development of their enterprises. This study uses the qualitative paradigm based on case studies on twenty-four women entrepreneurs in Peru.

The results show that women entrepreneurs seem not be a homogeneous group with unique characteristics, but they could be grouped based on their common experiences according to the phase in their life cycle when they decide to start an entrepreneurial activity and according to the factors that effected their decision to become entrepreneurs. The research identified six profiles that express the diverse routes taken by women to become entrepreneurs, called: Young Women with Employment Options, Growing Women with External Constraints, Consolidated Women with an Incomplete Career, Natural Young Women, Growing Women, and Consolidated Professional Women. Economic conditions in Peru may lead us to believe that this entrepreneurial activity in women is a result of economic needs, but the study concludes that achievement and autonomy are more frequent factors than economic circumstances in stimulating entrepreneurship in Peruvian women, and women in Peru seem to be influenced by factors that "pull" them to entrepreneurship and not only by circumstances that "push" them to choose an entrepreneurial activity.

The singularity of the document lies in the analysis of women entrepreneurs in Peru, a country with the highest entrepreneurial activity in the world, and adds more evidence of the characteristics of women entrepreneurs in a different context.

Figure 7.4 Example of an executive summary

To Rubén, Carolina and Julian

Figure 7.5 Example of a dedication

Dedication

The dedication is usually short. It should not include the word 'dedicated'; 'to' is sufficient. Extravagant dedications are a thing of the past. Keep in mind that everything that precedes the Table of Contents is not listed in the Table of Contents; only what is presented later is included. Figure 7.5 gives an example of a dedication.

Acronyms list

This list is necessary only if the author has defined new acronyms instead of using the commonly accepted ones. The acronyms are usually listed alphabetically. A thesis that includes many foreign or technical terms that are unfamiliar to the reader should include a list of those terms followed by its translation or definition. If all the definitions consist of phrases or short words, do not put a period at the end. Figure 7.6 shows an example of an acronyms list.

Table of Contents

The Table of Contents should list everything that comes after the Table of Contents. The Cover, the Executive summary, the Dedication and the Acknowledgements are placed before the Table of Contents; hence they should

Arrange
alphabetically

Abbreviations

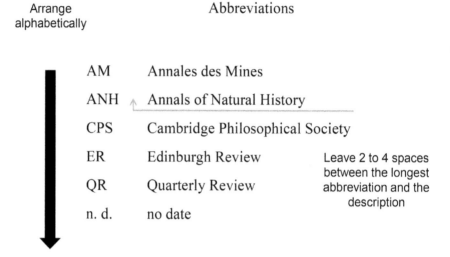

AM   Annales des Mines

ANH ∧ Annals of Natural History

CPS   Cambridge Philosophical Society

ER   Edinburgh Review

QR   Quarterly Review

n. d.   no date

Leave 2 to 4 spaces
between the longest
abbreviation and the
description

Figure 7.6 Example of an acronyms list

not be listed. Figure 7.7 depicts an example of a Table of Contents applicable to a qualitative study based on a case study, where the entire structure of the research paper is clearly shown.

List of tables

According to the references and writing style of the American Psychological Association (APA), any form of presentation used in the documents must be named either a table or a figure, not a graph or chart. According to APA standards: 'Tables usually show exact numerical values or textual information arranged in an orderly display of columns and rows, thus facilitating its comparison' (APA, 2009). The list of tables is intended to enumerate the tables included in the document.

When the tables are presented in the text of a document, the following recommendations should be followed:

a) Table titles should be brief, clear and explanatory.
b) In the text, the table title should be placed above the table, in the upper left margin under the word 'Table' (with an uppercase initial) with the correlative number (tables should be numbered sequentially with Arabic numerals in the text). For example: Table 1, Table 2, Table 3, etc.
c) For in-text table citation, the correct format is the following: 'According to Table 1 ...'. Note that the initial is capitalized when it is cited in the text.
d) A common error is to write 'the following Table, the Table below'. This is an incorrect way to cite the tables, always cite the Table with the corresponding correlative number.

Figure 7.7 Table of Contents of a research paper: an example based on case study methodology

Appendix 7.A includes a complete list of tables. Figure 7.8 shows an example of a list of tables.

List of Tables	
Table 1. *Profile of the Informants*	107
Table 2. *Informants Rate of Response*	109

Figure 7.8 Example of a list of tables in a research paper

Figure 7.9 Example of a list of figures in a research paper

List of figures

'A figure may be a chart, a graph, a photograph, a drawing, or any other illustration or non-textual depiction' (APA, 2009, p. 125). The list of figures is intended to enumerate the figures included in the document.

When the figures are presented in the text of a document, the following recommendations should be followed:

a) The title of the figure should be brief, clear and explanatory.
b) In the text, the figure title should be placed above the figure, in the upper left margin, under the word Figure (with an uppercase initial) with the correlative number (figures should be numbered sequentially with Arabic numerals in the text). For example: Figure 1, Figure 2, Figure 3, etc.
c) For in-text figure citation, the correct format is the following: 'According to Figure 1 …'. Note that the initial is capitalized when is cited in the text.
d) A common error is to write 'the following figure, the figure below'. This is an incorrect way to cite the figures, always cite the Figure and the corresponding correlative number.

Appendix 7.A includes a complete list of figures. Figure 7.9 shows an example of a list of figures.

The text

The text is the most important part of the document, as it represents the development of the author's proposals and criteria as a result of the research. The text should follow a logical, truthful and consistent sequence, and include references written in accordance with the style guidelines of the academic institution.

The text in research papers consists of five parts:

a) Introduction
b) Literature review
c) Method
d) Analysis and discussion of results
e) Conclusions and recommendations.

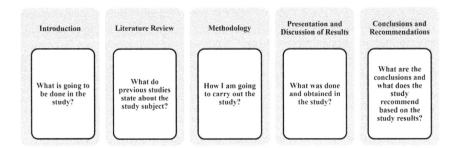

Figure 7.10 Structure of the text in a research paper

Each part has a specific purpose in the research process, as explained below (see Figure 7.10).

Introduction

The introduction aims to show what is to be done in the study; it explains in detail the background; defines the problem and purpose of the study, and its importance and nature; and specifies the research questions, the used theoretical framework, the definition of terms, the assumptions, and the limitations and delimitations. This introductory chapter, Chapter 1, always ends with an appropriate summary of the aspects covered in the chapter. The chapter has no conclusions, as none can be drawn based on what is presented.

Chapter 8 presents in detail the structure of an introduction chapter and gives a complete example of the information that should be included.

Literature review

This chapter aims to present the previous literature related to the study and to identify the gaps in the literature.

The literature review presents the current state of knowledge on a specific topic as an organized compendium that identifies, collects, analyses and contrasts information from complex arguments and conclusions on that topic. A review of the literature provides: (a) a critical analysis of related studies; (b) the relevant and irrelevant aspects of literature; and (c) conclusions of complex arguments developed on the specific topic. The literature review always begins with the literature map (also called a literature review matrix). The purpose of this matrix is to provide an approach to the object of study that clearly identifies the principal investigators and their respective contributions, the main aspects investigated, its variation over time, and an overall picture of the most relevant features of the situation or phenomenon under analysis.

Then, as many headings and paragraphs are included as are necessary. The chapter should end with a summary of the covered topics and the main conclusions of the chapter. The conclusions should reflect the gaps in the study literature, thus justifying the need for the study.

In Chapter 9, the structure of a literature review chapter is presented in detail, together with a complete example of the information to be considered in such a chapter.

Method

This chapter presents an explanation of the research method, and aims to show how the study is going to be carried out. It includes in great detail the following aspects of the method:

a)   explanation of the research design;
b)   justification of the selected study design based on the theoretical elements that supported the decision to choose that design;
c)   procedures used to select the cases;
d)   procedures used to collect the data;
e)   cases protocol;
f)   presentation of the instruments, as well as the procedure for their design and development;
g)   presentation of the agreed informed consent;
h)   procedures for data recording;
i)   procedures for data analysis and interpretation;
j)   strategies to ensure the validity and reliability of data;
k)   chapter summary.

Presentation and discussion of the results

This chapter, as its name implies, has two parts: (a) the presentation of the research results; and (b) discussion of the results obtained by comparing them with the studies included in the literature review chapter.

This is unquestionably the most important part of the document as it describes the purpose of the study. The presented results should answer clearly and directly the research questions posed in the introduction.

These two sections in research papers should be given careful consideration. They are usually organized with the same number of subheadings and research questions. For each question, the results are presented (in qualitative studies) in tables showing the frequency and then these results are discussed. Students often make mistakes in this chapter, as they confuse the presentation of the results with the discussion, leading to this chapter being presented in a disorganized and incomprehensible manner.

Conclusions and recommendations

The conclusions and recommendations are the final part of the text. The conclusions are those statements which derive directly from the analysis; they should not add additional information to the paper. The recommendations relate to the possible research extensions that may be performed and they suggest actions that must be taken. The recommendations are included after the conclusions, on a separate page.

This chapter includes the following parts:

a)   conclusions;
b)   theoretical contributions of the study, that is, the contribution to the theory;
c)   practical contributions, that's is, the contribution to business practice;
d)   limitations of the study;
e)   practical recommendations derived from the study and oriented to business practice;
f)   recommendations for future research studies derived from the conclusions made in the same study.

Students often confuse what the findings mean and instead of concluding in this section they present a summary of the data or a summary of the results of the investigation. However, the conclusions should not include data from the literature review, nor the results. Students must include the outcome of the study analysis. The conclusions should clearly answer the questions posed in the study.

Final section

The final section of a research paper has two parts: (a) References, and (b) Appendices.

Reference list

The references contain the source of the information cited in the text. Hence, they must be clear, organized and concise, and they should allow easy location of the source for further information or simply for verification purposes. They are very important because they show the intellectual honesty of the author when citing other authors who have contributed to the study.

The references should be written in accordance with the adopted references style. In the case of the social sciences, the preferred style is usually that of the American Psychological Association (APA). The citation style can be found in the *Publication Manual of the American Psychological Association* (6th edition). Additional information can be obtained from the website http://www.apastyle. org, which includes tutorials and FAQs.

Appendices

The appendices include all the relevant material that provides further information about the document, but that is not relevant enough to be included in the main text. Some examples of appendices are: surveys or questionnaires, additional tables or figures, additional information, among others.

It is very important to note that the term Annexes should not be used. In addition, the appendices must be numbered with letters not numbers. For example: Appendix A, Appendix B, and so on. They can be single or double spaced, depending on the nature of the material (see Figure 7.11).

Appendix A: Theoretical Framework
Appendix B: Preliminary Research Conducted into Individual Aspects
Appendix C: Preliminary Research Conducted into Processes
Appendix D: Field Notes Forms
Appendix E: Informed Consent
Appendix F: Classification Questions

Appendix G: Interview Guide
Appendix H: Case Protocol
Appendix I: Maps
Appendix J: Profile of Informants
Appendix K: Results of Analysed Cases

Figure 7.11 Appendices in a research paper: a case study example

References

American Psychological Association (APA) (2009). *Publication Manual of the American Psychological Association* (6th edition).

Avolio Alecchi, B. (2010). El Perfil de las Mujeres Empresarias en el Perú. [An Exploratory Study of the Profile of Women Entrepreneurs in Peru]. DBA thesis, Pontifical Catholic University of Peru.

Cremmins, E. (1996). *The Art of Abstracting* (2nd edition). Arlington, VA: Information Resources Press.

Koopman, P. (October, 1997). How to write an abstract. Carnegie Mellon University, Pittsburgh, PA. Available at: http://www.soest.hawaii.edu/GG/FACULTY/conrad/classes/GG610_F11/How_to_Write_an_Abstract.pdf

Appendix 7.A: An example of preliminary pages

Maastricht School of Management

A profile of women entrepreneurs in Peru:
an exploratory study

Dissertation

To obtain the degree of Doctor of Business Administration at the Maastricht
School of Management
by

Beatrice E. Avolio Alecchi

Master of Philosophy, Maastricht School of Management
Born in Lima, Peru

A profile of women entrepreneurs in Peru:
an exploratory study
By
Beatrice E. Avolio Alecchi

The dissertation is approved by the Doctoral Supervisors:

Prof. Khaled Wahba
Maastricht School of Management, the Netherlands

Reader:
Prof. Fred Phillips
Maastricht School of Management, the Netherlands

External evaluators:

Abstract

The study identifies the profile of women entrepreneurs in Peru by exploring qualitatively their demographic characteristics; their education, work and family backgrounds; their administrative skills; the nature of their enterprises; the driving factors to become entrepreneurs; and the obstacles for the development of their enterprises. This study uses the qualitative paradigm based on case studies on twenty-four women entrepreneurs in Peru.

The results show that women entrepreneurs seem not be a homogeneous group with unique characteristics, but they could be grouped based on their common experiences according to the phase in their life cycle when they decide to start an entrepreneurial activity and according to the factors that effected their decision to become entrepreneurs. Research identified six profiles that express the diverse routes taken by women to become entrepreneurs, called: Young Women with Employment Options, Growing Women with External Constraints, Consolidated Women with an Incomplete Career, Natural Young Women, Growing Women under Way and Consolidated Professional Women. Economic conditions in Peru may lead us to believe that this entrepreneurial activity in women is a result of economic needs, but the study concludes that *achievement and autonomy* are more frequent factors than economic circumstances in stimulating entrepreneurship in Peruvian women, and women in Peru seem to be influenced by factors that 'pull' them to entrepreneurship and not only by circumstances that 'push' them to choose an entrepreneurial activity.

The singularity of the document lies in the analysis of women entrepreneurs in Peru, a country with the highest entrepreneurial activity in the world, and adds more evidence of the characteristics of women entrepreneurs in a different context.

Dedication

To my children, Renato and Raffaella, my life great treasures. They are my source of inspiration for everything I undertake in life.

Acknowledgements

My cordial thanks to Prof. Khaled Wahba for his dedication, his prompt responses along the course of the research proposal and his contribution in developing my understanding on the subject of study. His permanent support and constructive feedback allowed me to complete this study.

My very special thanks to Prof. Fernando D'Alessio, for his tutorship, assistance and permanent motivation to fulfil my professional goals. I believe that without his guidance and direction, this work would have never been completed.

Table of Contents

5 Conclusions and Recommendations **273**

List of Tables

List of Figures

8   The introduction

Chapter 1 of a research paper is the introduction. The introduction aims to show what is to be done in the study; that is, it explains in detail the background; defines the problem and purpose of the study, and its importance and nature; and specifies the research questions, the theoretical framework, the definition of terms, the assumptions, and the limitations and delimitations. This first chapter always ends with an appropriate summary of the aspects covered in the chapter. The chapter has no conclusions, as none can be drawn based on what is presented.

The contents of the introduction will be explained and presented in detail. An example based on a qualitative paradigm of the case study will also be included (Yin, 2003).

Initial paragraphs

Each chapter should start with a few introductory paragraphs that explain what the chapter is about. The first paragraph immediately follows the chapter title and it should be carefully written as it is the first thing the reader will read; it must be clear and concise, and engage the reader. This paragraph should arouse curiosity in the reader so that they want to continue reading the document. These initial paragraphs are followed by heading 1.1: Background.

The following example of some initial paragraphs is taken from Avolio's dissertation (2010):

Chapter 1: Introduction

During the last decades, major efforts have been carried out all over the world to stimulate the development of entrepreneurial activity, owing to the acknowledgement that enterprise creation is related to economic growth and employment generation (Weeks and Seiler, 2001). In order to understand the phenomenon of entrepreneurial activity, the first step

(Continued)

(Continued)

to explore must be the entrepreneur's background, as well as the motivations that generate the creation of enterprises, given that the success of an enterprise depends on the person's initiative to create a viable business (Mitchell, 2004). Knowing the factors that motivate a person to start an entrepreneurial career is important in stimulating the development of entrepreneurial activity.

Entrepreneurship refers to the 'activities associated with being an entrepreneur' (HarperCollins, 2003) and it is a relatively recent research area. However, it has been one of the fields of research with the largest expansion. Specifically, since 1970, there has been a growing interest in the entrepreneurial activity of women in the world, owing to the great growth in business start-ups by females and based on the assumption that, women encounter difficulties in starting and operating a business which are different from those faced by men (Neider, 1987). Women entrepreneurs have been identified as a 'major force for innovation and job creation' (Organization for economic Cooperation and Development [OECD], quoted by Orhan and Scott, 2001, p. 232).

Even though entrepreneurship has become one of the fastest growing fields of research over the last decades, most of the studies were developed and tested on samples of men entrepreneurs, and in developed countries. Diverse authors consider that applying results from studies on men entrepreneurs to women, and applying results obtained from developed countries to other realities, is inadequate (Brush and Bird, 2002; Carter and Cannon, 1992; Minniti, Arenius and Langowitz, 2005; Mitchell, 2004; Weeks and Seiler, 2001; Zapalska, 1997). In Latin America in particular, there has been limited research on the role played by women and there are very concrete facts regarding women and their enterprises. The cultural differences of Latin American countries with regard to developed countries make Latin American women entrepreneurs' experiences unique. Some studies in developed countries have explored women entrepreneurs' possible motivations, and suggest a wide range of reasons, but such reasons have not yet been integrated into a model that explains the relationship between women backgrounds and the factors that stimulated them to become entrepreneurs. Besides, studies investigating why women become entrepreneurs do not integrate these factors according to their nature.

This study uses a qualitative approach to explore women's backgrounds (demographic, educational, work and family backgrounds) and their relation to the factors that have motivated women to become entrepreneurs, in order to develop an integrated model. It also explores the nature of the enterprises owned by women and the obstacles faced in order to develop the profile of women entrepreneurs. This study uses the case of women entrepreneurs in Peru. Using the Peruvian case to increase knowledge about women entrepreneurs is appropriate because, as the Global Entrepreneurship Monitor; Peru 2004–2005 points out, Peru is the country with the highest rate of Total Entrepreneurial Activity rate (TEA) in the world (Serida, Borda, Nakamatsu, Morales and Yamakawa, 2005). TAE measures the percentage of adults between 18 and 64 years that own all or part of a business for less than 42 months and includes incipient enterprises as well as new enterprises. An enterprise is considered incipient if the proprietors of all or part of a business express paying wages or salaries for not more than three months or mention having taken specific actions to start the business. An enterprise is considered new if the proprietors of all or part of a business they actively manage have paid remunerations for more than three months but less than 42 (Serida *et al.*, 2005). This study does not intend to give all answers related to women entrepreneurs, but presents an important contribution to the knowledge of entrepreneurial activity in subjects and fields that current literature has not yet addressed thoroughly.

The problem of the study, as well as the purpose, importance, nature and questions of the study are put forward in this chapter. The conceptual framework, assumptions, limitations and delimitations of the study are also defined.

1.1. Background

[And so on ...]

Definition of the problem

The definition of the research problem is perhaps the least easily understood section when defining a study and writing a research paper. However, it is essential to define the problem clearly and accurately.

The study subject is often confused with the research problem. The best way to explain the definition of the problem is to use an example. Assume that the life cycle of businesses in a country has been decreasing in the last years, which is detrimental to the economic development, employment generation, and the production level of that particular country. One of the possible causes of business mortality could be the lack of strategic planning skills within the organizations. Therefore, you want to investigate the business strategic management level in that country, as it is possible that this may be one of the major causes of mortality. In this sense, the problem is the mortality level of businesses and the subject is related to the strategic management in these organizations.

The following example of a problem definition is taken from Avolio's dissertation (2010):

Definition of the Problem

According to the *Global Entrepreneurship Monitor: Peru 2004–2005* (Serida et al., 2005), it is estimated that around 6,325,000 Peruvians were involved in an entrepreneurial initiative in 2004; approximately 3,065,000 of whom were women (48.5 per cent), representing the highest Total Entrepreneurial Activities rates (TEA) out of the 34 countries included in the study: 40.3 per cent of the general TEA and 39.1 per cent of the female TEA. Both indicators show the level of entrepreneurial activity of the population in general and women's important participation. However, the same source shows that Peru holds one of the last places in the study (only before Hungary, Ecuador and Japan) with regard to institutional support for women entrepreneurs, which shows that:

> Institutionality in the country would not be motivating or making the development of these entrepreneurships sufficiently easier, especially in the stages of life when women must set aside a lot of their time and effort to their traditional role inside the family. (p. 62)

The existing lack of institutional support for female entrepreneurial activity represents a problem in promoting their development in the country. In order to design support programmes and policies aimed at women, it is necessary to analyse in depth the women entrepreneurship phenomenon. That is why the development of a profile of women entrepreneurs will provide knowledge that will make it possible to develop support programmes and policies directed to encourage their capacities, increase the probabilities of success of their entrepreneurial effort, develop a better environment that promotes their entrepreneurial activity and help generate a more plural and modern society, besides promoting the country's economic development.

Background

This next section describes the background to the study, and consists of a brief summary of its relevant aspects. The background must show the desirability of the study and the context.

Some points to be considered regarding the background include:

a)   the background must have a maximum of four pages;
b)   usually it does not include tables or graphics, only text;
c)   it must provide clear information about the study subject;
d)   the writing style should be concise and clear, and to the point.

The following example of a background section is taken from Avolio's dissertation (2010):

Background

It is a fact that women entrepreneurial activity in the world is increasing. According to the Centre for Women's Business Research (2006a), in the United States, 40.2 per cent of the private enterprises are, in 50 per cent or more, the property of women. Internationally, the growth in the number of enterprises run by women has followed similar patterns to that of the United States. There are few statistics in Latin America that quantify women's economic contribution, but it is estimated that between 25 per cent and 35 per cent of employers and self-employed people in Latin America and the Caribbean are women (Weeks and Seiler, 2001).

Internationally, research into women entrepreneurs is growing, especially in developed countries. In developing countries, especially in Latin America, the studies are few and there is limited information about the role played by women entrepreneurs. This represents a problem in understanding the phenomenon of women entrepreneurs, as social, work and family structures vary considerably in developing countries. For this reason, models based on developed countries are considered imprecise for understanding women entrepreneurs in other contexts. It is possible that the weakness or absence of entrepreneurship development strategies in the public programme of most Latin American countries is due to the lack of knowledge about entrepreneurial activity (Kantis, Ishida and Komori, 2002). Because of that, it is necessary to first analyse the diverse economic and social structures, and the theories about women entrepreneurs based on developed countries before applying them in other contexts: '… theories regarding women entrepreneurs based on developed countries need to be carefully examined before being applied to non-OECD and developing countries'. (Hisrich and Ayse Öztürk, 1999, p. 114).

This study focuses on the case of women entrepreneurs in Peru. Statistical and qualitative information on women entrepreneurs is scarce in Peru. Peru has the highest Female Total Entrepreneurial Activity rate in the world (39.1 per cent), according to the Global Entrepreneurship Monitor: 2004 Report on Women and Entrepreneurship (GEM) study carried out in 34 countries by Minniti *et al.* (2005) for the Babson's College Centre for Women's Leadership, in the United States. It has also the highest Total Entrepreneurial Activity rate (40.3 per cent) registered by the GEM study since its creation in 2000 (Serida *et al.*, 2005, p. 21).

(Continued)

(Continued)

Of the Peruvian population 50.1 per cent (National Institute of Statistics and Computer Sciences [INEI], 2006b) and 21.4 per cent of the heads of household are women (INEI, 2006a). In 1981, only 26 out of every 100 Peruvian women of working age were currently working, representing 24.6 per cent of the Economically Active Population – EAP (Blondet and Montero, 1994, p. 207); and this number increased to 61 out of every 100 by the year 2004, increasing to 43.8 per cent women participation in the country's economic activity (INEI, 2005a, p. 273). The growth in women's economic activity is also made evident through their participation in the tax base: the number of women registered as tax payers doubled in the 2002–2007 period, when they went from representing 37 per cent of the individual's tax base to representing 40 per cent of the total (Vejarano, 2007).

The specific study for Peru, Global Entrepreneurship Monitor: Peru 2004–2005 (Serida *et al.*, 2005), estimates that around 6,325,000 Peruvians are involved in an entrepreneurial initiative, 3,065,000 of whom are women (48.5 per cent). The Female Entrepreneurial Activity rate / Male Entrepreneurial Activity rate ratio is 0.94, the highest value of all countries included in the study. However, Peru has the second highest rate of enterprise mortality (11.5 per cent) in Latin America after Ecuador (Serida *et al.*, 2005).

Out of the formal enterprises in Peru, 98.3 per cent are micro-enterprises or small enterprises, which contribute 42.1 per cent of the Domestic Gross Product (Centre for Small and Micro Enterprise Promotion [PROMPYME], 2005a) and give work to more than one million people, 32.8 per cent of whom are women (PROMPYME, 2005b, p. 28). The informal activity in Peru reaches higher levels than formal activity: it is estimated that 74 per cent of the enterprises are informal, and that they employ 6.2 million people, 42.3 per cent of whom are women (PROMPYME, 2005b).

These data show the importance of women's entrepreneurial activity in Peru, a situation similar to what happens in other countries of Latin America and the world. However, in Latin America, and especially in Peru, there are very few studies about the phenomenon of women entrepreneurs.

Purpose of the study

The purpose of the study is the research objective; it must be expressed clearly and consistently. Researchers probably spend more time on the clear and precise writing of the purpose of the study than on any other section.

In some cases, it is advisable to establish the general purpose of the study and also the specific purposes of the study.

The following example of a purpose of the study section is taken from Avolio's dissertation (2010):

Purpose of the Study

The purpose of this qualitative study is to try to identify the profile of Peruvian women entrepreneurs through qualitative exploration of: (a) their demographic characteristics; (b) their educational, work and family backgrounds; (c) their administrative/management skills; (d) the nature of their enterprises; (e) the factors that have motivated them to become entrepreneurs; and (f) the principal obstacles in starting and managing the growth of their enterprises; all of this by collecting information on women entrepreneurs in Peru.

The study has five goals. The first one is to explore the characteristics of women entrepreneurs (demographic, educational, work and family backgrounds), their administrative/managing abilities, and the nature of their enterprises. The second is to explain the factors that have motivated the women to choose entrepreneurship. The third one is to explain the obstacles women face in their enterprises. The fourth is to propose a conceptual framework to explain why women chose entrepreneurial activities, taking their backgrounds and factors that motivated them to become entrepreneurs into account. The fifth goal is to identify the profile of women entrepreneurs in Peru by developing a typology that takes into account their backgrounds, the factors that motivated them to entrepreneurial activities and the obstacles they face in developing their enterprises.

Importance of the study

The importance of the study refers to why it is worthwhile to develop the study. It should provide clearly and concisely enough arguments to justify the research, in terms of a theoretical or practical contribution.

The following example of an importance of the study section is taken from Avolio's dissertation (2010):

Importance of the Study

Studying the profile of women entrepreneurs is important for several reasons. In the first place, previous studies show that promoting women through the ownership of private enterprises is a beneficial economic strategy: the creation of enterprises promotes economic growth and provides employment opportunities for their owners and their employees, and also gives economic opportunities to women to improve their social, education and health situations, as well as those of their families (Weeks and Seiler, 2001).

(Continued)

(Continued)

Second, between 25 per cent and 35 per cent of formal enterprises in Latin America and the Caribbean are operated and managed by women. In spite of the limited and far from perfect information available, women entrepreneurs are not only an important part of Latin American entrepreneurial activity, but their participation is also growing (Weeks and Seiler, 2001).

Third, the studies on women entrepreneurs in developing countries and in Latin America are scarce, and in an exploratory phase. In Peru, the statistical and qualitative information on women entrepreneurs is scarce. This lack of research on women entrepreneurs represents a problem in understanding the phenomenon and makes the design of support programmes and policies that promote the creation of enterprises by women difficult. According to Minniti *et al.* (2005):

> When women are unable to develop all their economic potential, the whole economy suffers. A better understanding of the potential contribution of women in the entrepreneurial field would allow designing better programs directed to increase their participation in the market. Besides providing important knowledge on the entrepreneurial process, understanding and supporting the entrepreneurial behavior of women will have a positive impact in the wellness of countries and in social equity. (p. 36)

This study provides important information and knowledge for obtaining the profile of women entrepreneurs based on the Peruvian case, and contributes to the knowledge of their needs and characteristics so that support programmes and government policies may be properly directed to promote a more favourable environment for the development of women's entrepreneurial spirit.

Nature of the study

The nature of the study describes concisely the selected research plan. It must include, at least, the following information:

a) purpose (exploratory, descriptive, explicative)
b) approach (qualitative, quantitative)
c) strategy (case study, grounded theory, ethnography, etc.)
d) strategy justification
e) instruments
f) sampling
g) data collection
h) data analysis.

The following example of a nature of the study section is taken from Avolio's dissertation (2010):

Nature of the Study

The study has used a qualitative approach to explore the profile of women entrepreneurs. The qualitative strategy used is that of multiple case studies under a holistic design. The qualitative strategy used is appropriate for the following reasons: (a) it allows appropriate answers to the questions *what* and *why* (Yin, 2003); (b) there is no control over the women's decision to become entrepreneurs (Yin, 2003); (c) it allows gathering knowledge on complex, sensitive and personal aspects, such as the decision to become an entrepreneur (Stevenson, 1990). Multiple cases have been examined, as they give greater evidence than a single case, produce a more complete study and increase the reliability of the results (Yin, 2003).

The population of women entrepreneurs comprises those women who own 50 per cent or more of a formal enterprise, are actively involved in its operation and generate employment for themselves and for others, regardless of how the ownership was obtained. As there are no databases of women entrepreneurs in Peru, several sources have been used to identify potential participants for the study: women entrepreneurs that have asked for a loan from specialized banks, information published in newspapers, referrals from personal contacts and referrals from the women entrepreneurs themselves. The sample was built using a combination of the *snowball* and *maximum variation* techniques. The sample has been carefully structured to reflect the diversity of situations faced by women entrepreneurs, considering the following dimensions: age, marital status, educational level, economic sector of the enterprise, way the owner-ship was acquired, time of operation and size of the enterprise. The data has been collected principally through in-depth interviews, on several sessions, in several places. The interviews were open, conducted using a guide. The interviews were taped and transcribed, and an appropriate chain of evidence in the analysis has been maintained through the documentation of the interview, Informed Consent, the field notes, the researcher's report and the protocol of the case. The information has been codified, categorized and analysed using *analytical induction* (Strauss and Corbin, 1998) and the procedures suggested by Miles and Huberman (1994) to analyse qualitative information. The *Atlas* software has been used to process information, which allows the evidence to be kept clear between narratives and codifying the information.

Research questions

The research questions are related to the purpose of the study. The questions are the inquiries that the research must answer in order to achieve the purpose of the study. The questions have to be carefully posed, as they constitute the basis of the research.

The following example of a research questions section is taken from Avolio's dissertation (2010):

Research Questions

The research question for the study is: What is the profile of women entrepreneurs in Peru?

The study is a qualitative exploration of the women entrepreneurs' profile in Peru, in which we try to determine the following: (a) the demographic characteristics of women entrepreneurs; (b) the educational, work and family backgrounds of women entrepreneurs; (c) the administrative/managing skills of women entrepreneurs; (d) the characteristics of enterprises owned in 50 per cent or more by women; (e) the factors that have motivated women to become entrepreneurs; and (f) the principal obstacles to start and develop an enterprise owned by women?

Propositions

The research questions are related to the propositions. The research questions are the inquiries that the researcher should respond to throughout the study. On the other hand, the propositions are the predictions made about the answers to these questions. In quantitative studies, the propositions are called hypotheses. In qualitative studies, they are called propositions.

Not all studies are required to have propositions; there are studies that do not need to have propositions as their scope is exploratory (Yin, 2003).

Theoretical framework

The theoretical framework refers to the theories and concepts to be used in the research process. The literature review (Chapter 2) should be developed first to define the theoretical framework. However, the introduction usually presents a summary of the theoretical or conceptual framework of the study.

The theoretical framework, in addition to the narrative explanation, generally includes a figure that helps to illustrate the relationship of the used concepts and theories.

The following example of a theoretical framework section is taken from Avolio's dissertation (2010):

Theoretical Framework

The theoretical approach is used as conceptual framework to collect and analyse information case studies. According to Yin (2003), the use of theory before collecting information is an essential step, even if it is an exploratory study.

'The use of theory, in using case study, is not only an immense aid in defining the appropriate research design and data collection, but it also becomes the main vehicle for generalizing the results of the case study'. (Yin. 2003, p. 33).

The conceptual framework presented is a modified version of the Orhan and Scott model (2001), considering the Cooper (1981) and Goffee and Scase (1985) studies. Cooper (1981) identified that the reason for creating a new enterprise is influenced by the person's background, which affects their motivations, perceptions, knowledge and abilities; by the organizations for which the person has worked before, the nature of which influence the location, nature and line of business of the new enterprises; and by the factors external to the individual and the organization, which generate a more or less favourable environment for starting a new enterprise.

Orhan and Scott (2001) developed a model of motivational factors of women entrepreneurs by using the qualitative paradigm in 25 women entrepreneurs. They identified seven types of motives women have to become entrepreneurs, called: *agreed dynasty, with no other choice, entrepreneur by choice, natural succession, forced entrepreneur, informed entrepreneur* and *pure entrepreneur*. The results do not reinforce the assumption that most women become entrepreneurs because of economic needs.

The model proposed as theoretical perspective considers two dimensions: (a) the background of women before becoming entrepreneurs, and (b) their motives to become entrepreneurs. The dimensions of the model, related to the background of women, were defined into two categories in the Goffee and Scase studies (1985), according to the willingness of the women to accept their traditional gender roles: (a) women with high values for traditional gender roles, and (b) women with low values for traditional gender roles. Women in the first category deeply support a culture of male domination, which discloses a low level of education of the woman, or education directed towards typically female activities, such as nurse, housewife, secretary, assistant, etc., with very low opportunities for professional growth. The second category refers to the gradual entrance of women into professional areas that used to be considered male activities, directed towards a managing and executive level, such as manager, professional, executive or entrepreneur. The low support to the traditional role is evident in a university or college education, in professional areas such as business, law, medicine, engineering or also when the personal activity shows a high level of accomplishment and originality.

The motivations to become entrepreneurs consider the *push, pull* and situational factors. The *push* factors are those that have driven the woman to become an entrepreneur, and are related to situations such as dissatisfaction with a paid job with an unfair remuneration or lack of potential for career development; the problems in finding a dependent job; the need to have a flexible schedule because of other responsibilities, such as taking care of the children and the

(Continued)

(Continued)

home; insufficient family income that forces the woman to partially or totally assume the economic responsibility for the family; or the existence of a family business where the presence of the woman is needed (Orhan and Scott, 2001).

The *pull* factors refer to situations that motivate women to voluntarily become entrepreneurs, and these are related to independence, self-satisfaction, entrepreneurial inclinations and the desire for social status and power. The situational factors refer to the event where a woman becomes an entrepreneur by inheriting a family business, by existing models that provide support or help in the entrepreneurial project. The dimensions of the model, its definition and categorization are detailed in Appendix A. None of the categories on the model is mutually excluding, and there may be several classifications for each woman entrepreneur.

Theoretical framework: factors related to women's decisions to become entrepreneurs

Factors	Concept	Source of evidence
Dimension 1: High attachment to the traditional role of women	Long rooted to a culture of male dominance revealed through a low educational level, education toward activities typically feminine such as housekeeper or nursing, secretary or housewife, with little probability of professional growth.	Educational level related with activities traditionally feminine (secretary, nursing, no education) Work experience related with traditionally feminine activities (secretary, assistant, employees, housewife)
Dimension 2: Low attachment to the traditional role of women	The progressive entry to professional areas traditionally reserved as male activities, oriented to a managerial or executive level. Additionally, when women wish to reach patterns similar to male patterns, by acknowledging their own identity, regardless of gender stereotypes. It is shown through university or higher education, in professional areas such as business, law, medicine, engineering, or also, when the personal activity shows a high level of achievement and originality.	Educational level related with activities traditionally not reserved for women (business, law, medicine, engineering, etc.). Work experience related with activities traditionally not reserved for women (managers, professionals, executives, entrepreneurs)

Orhan, M. and Scott, D. (2001). Why women enter into entrepreneurship: An explanatory model. *Journal of Management Review*, 16(5/6), 232–242.

Definition of terms

The definition of terms classifies the terms used in the study. Depending on the nature and complexity of the study, this section may be extensive. The definitions included in this section should include the references from which the different terms have been obtained.

The following example of a definition of terms section is taken from Avolio's dissertation (2010):

Definition of Terms

The term *entrepreneurship* is defined as: *'The state of being an entrepreneur or the activities associated with being an entrepreneur'* (HarperCollins, 2003). There is no agreement on the translation of the term *entrepreneurship* into Spanish. Some use *espíritu empresarial* (HarperCollins, 2005), *empresarialidad* (Argentina), or *emprendedorismo* (Brazil and works carried out by the Inter-American Development Bank) (United States Agency of International Development [USAID], 2005). In this study, we use *emprendimiento* to refer to the concept of *entrepreneurship*, that is to say, *to the activities associated with being an entrepreneur.*

The term *empresa* comes from the English term *enterprise* (HarperCollins, 2005), and is defined as: *'An organization, especially a business, or a difficult and important plan, especially one that will earn money'* (Cambridge University Press, 2008); and as 'Unidad de organización dedicada a actividades industriales, mercantiles o de prestación de servicios con fines lucrativos' (Real Academia de la Lengua, 2001) [Organizational unit dedicated to industrial, mercantile or service rendering activities]. An organization is an: 'Asociación de personas regulada por un conjunto de normas en función de determinados fines' (Real Academia de la Lengua, 2001) [Association of persons ruled by a set of rules, according to specific ends]. The term *negocio* is equivalent to the English term *business* (HarperCollins, 2005) and refers to: *'The activity of buying and selling goods and services, or a particular company that does this, or work you do to earn money'* (Cambridge University Press, 2008); and as: 'Aquello que es objeto o materia de una ocupación lucrativa' (Real Academia de la Lengua, 2001) [The object or matter of a profitable occupation]. This study uses the term *empresa* to refer to the concept of *enterprise*, that is to say, *to the organizations dedicated to industrial, commercial or service activities with profit-making ends*; and the term *negocio* to refer to the concept of *business*, that is, *that which is the object of a profitable occupation, without necessarily implying an organization.*

The term *empresario* is equivalent to the English term *entrepreneur* (HarperCollins, 2005) and is defines as: *'Someone who starts their own*

(Continued)

(Continued)

business, especially when this involves risks' (Cambridge University Press, 2008), or as: 'Titular propietario o directivo de una industria, negocio o empresa' (Real Academia de la Lengua, 2001) [Titular owner or member of the board of directors of an industry, business or enterprise]. For Steinhoff and Burguess (1989, quoted by Smith-Hunter, 2003), the entrepreneur is a 'person who organizes, operates and takes the risks involved in operating an enterprise' (p. 14). Schwartz (1976) defined the entrepreneur as 'an innova- tive individual that creates and builds a business that did not exist before' (p. 47). Hisrich and Brush (1986) defined an entrepreneur as the person who 'creates something different of value dedicating the necessary time and effort, taking the financial, psychological and social risks, and receiving the monetary rewards and personal satisfaction' (p. 4). Bennett and Dann (2000) defined the entrepreneur as 'the person who has established the enterprise as a new business, where the development of the enterprise is sought for the primary reasons of obtaining profits and satisfaction' (p. 78).

According to these definitions, entrepreneur can only refer, *strictu sensu*, to a person who founds an enterprise or business. From a wider perspective, it can refer to the ownership of enterprises, regardless of the way such own- ership was obtained (foundation, purchase, inheritance) (Hisrich and Brush, 1986). According to Cooper and Dunkelberg (1981), a person may have also become an enterprise owner in several ways: (a) by founding an enterprise; (b) by purchasing the enterprise from a person outside the family; (c) by family succession, including the purchase of the enterprise from a family member; or (d) by promotion or incorporation to the enterprise by the owners. The founda- tion of an enterprise implies taking personal risks and the capacity to innovate when conceiving and creating a business, and taking the initiative to estab- lish something new. The purchase of an enterprise also implies taking risks and requires initiative to find and agree to buying an enterprise; however, it needs less creativity and vision to detect opportunities or to obtain the neces- sary resources to create an enterprise. To become the owner of an enterprise by heritage, promotion or incorporation into the enterprise as part owner implies even fewer personal risks (even though the obligation, reputation and other personal aspects may be involved) and does not require the innovation needed to obtain the necessary resources to create an enterprise (even though it may require a lot of inventiveness to expand the already existing enterprise).

This study defines *woman entrepreneur* as a *woman who owns an enter- prise (regardless of the way the ownership was obtained), who is actively involved in its operation as manager or administrator, and generates employment for herself and for others.*

This study makes no difference regarding the way the ownership of the enterprises was generated as, from a larger definition, the entrepreneurship can refer to the creation and ownership of enterprises, regardless of the way ownership was obtained (Hisrich and Brush, 1986).

The definition of the term *woman entrepreneur* for this study implies the woman holds the position of manager and employer of her own enterprise. The term *gerente* or *administrador* is equivalent to the English term *manager* (HarperCollins, 2005) and it is defined as: '*To be responsible for controlling or organizing someone or something especially a business*' (Cambridge University Press, 2008) and as: 'Persona que lleva la gestión administrativa de una empresa o institución' (Real Academia de la Lengua, 2001) [Person who holds the administrative managing of an enterprise or institution]. The term *empleador* is equivalent to the English term *employer* (HarperCollins, 2005) and is defined as: '*A person or organization that employs people*' (Cambridge University Press, 2008).

The term *emprendedor* is equivalent to the English term *enterprising* (HarperCollins, 2003), and is defined as: '*Doing new and difficult things, especially things that will make money*' (Cambridge University Press, 2008); or as the person: 'Que emprende con resolución acciones dificultosas o azarosas' (Real Academia de la Lengua, 2001) [Who resolutely starts difficult or risky actions]. According to the definition, the term *enterprising* does not necessarily imply that the initiative has consolidated into the creation of an enterprise. The term *enterprising* is used in this study only to refer to the results of the Minniti *et al.* (2005) studies, which calculate the *Total Entrepreneurial Activity rate* and define *enterprising* as 'Any attempt of new businesses or creation of new enterprises, such as self-employment, reorganization of a business, or the expansion of an already existing business by an individual, group of individuals or an already established enterprise' (Serida *et al.*, 2005).

Based on the definition for the term *woman entrepreneur*, and considering the Bennet and Dann (2000), Inman (2000), Lee-Gosselin and Grisé (1990) and Voeten (2002a) studies, the definition of *woman entrepreneur* has been built considering the following criteria: (a) have a formally operating enterprise at the time of the study, in order to consider only formal enterprises; (b) own 50 per cent or more of the enterprise, regardless of the way the ownership was obtained; (c) have more than two employees, in order to separate the study from self-employment; (d) their enterprises have been formally working for two years or more, in order to distinguish short-term opportunities from long-term commitments; (e) have an important role in the enterprise at the time of the study; (f) have a full-time job in the enterprise, in order to ensure women have a high commitment to their enterprises; (g) receive the majority of their income from the enterprise, in order to distinguish women entrepreneurs from those who do business eventually; and (h) be linked to the enterprise for at least two years.

Assumptions

The assumptions are those suppositions that are presumed to be true or real, but they have not been demonstrated as such in the study. The study is developed taking into consideration certain assumptions and these should be clarified in the introduction.

The following example of an assumptions section is taken from Avolio's dissertation (2010):

Assumptions

The study assumes that women entrepreneurs are different from men entrepreneurs in Peru in a series of important dimensions. Hisrich and Brush (1986) found that men and women entrepreneurs in the United States differ in their motivations, processes involved in starting their enterprises, administrative and entrepreneurial abilities, work backgrounds and problems they face. Minniti *et al.* (2005) found that the entrepreneurial attitudes of men and women are influenced by several of the same variables, but that these factors do not influence both genders in the same way or with the same intensity. Mitchell (2004) found that women entrepreneurs in South Africa have different problems than those faced by men entrepreneurs. Zapalska (1997) found that women entrepreneurs in the United States distinguish themselves from men entrepreneurs in the obstacles they face, the reasons to start a business, their objectives and factors each one perceives for success.

Limitations

The study limitations are the potential weaknesses of the study (Creswell, 2003) that are beyond the researcher's control. The limitations are related to the data collection and analysis research methods, such as the limitations of statistical procedures, surveys, generalization of data, etc.

The following example of a limitations section is taken from Avolio's dissertation (2010):

Limitations

The limitations of the study are: (a) no statistics generalizations are made on the population; (b) the data is collected based on in-depth interviews, and women may have not shared personal and deep reasons about their motives to establish an enterprise; (c) the reasons to become entrepreneurs, as well as the obstacles women entrepreneurs face are valued according to their perception on the motives to establish an enterprise; (d) the reasons to become entrepreneurs as well as the obstacles women entrepreneurs face are valued according to their perception, through the informant's discourse; (e) the definition of formality refers to the legal and tax aspects of the enterprises, that is to say, those enterprises that have legal economic activity, that operate as companies or individuals with entrepreneurial activity, are considered legal, although it does not mean that they comply with labour and tax standards; and (f) one of the difficulties of researching into women entrepreneurs is the lack of a database on which to build representative samples of women entrepreneurs in Peru, which is why the study uses a purpose sampling that diminishes the generalization of results.

Delimitations

The study delimitations determine the scope of the study (Creswell, 2003). These are defined by the researcher; they depend on his decision and control. For example, a common delimitation is related to the geographic scope of the study, which depends on the researcher's decision. It is important not only to set the delimitations but also to explain the reasons for these in the study.

The following example of a delimitations section is taken from Avolio's dissertation (2010):

Delimitations

The delimitations of the study are: (a) the study is done in Metropolitan Lima, and the results are only valid for this city; (b) the study only analyses the formal sector of women entrepreneurs; (c) there is not a generally accepted definition about what an woman entrepreneur is, the study defines her as *such woman who owns an enterprise (regardless of the way the ownership was obtained), is actively involved in its operation as manager or administrator, and generates employment for herself and for others*; (d) *self-employment* is excluded from the study because it is not considered an *enterprise*; and (e) the study considers enterprises with two or more years of legal operation, which can show a bias towards successful enterprises.

The study is conducted in Metropolitan Lima, as this city concentrates 29.7 per cent of the total population of Peru and 30.2 per cent of the Peruvian female population (INEI, 2006b), 47.9 per cent of the Domestic Gross Product (for the Department of Lima), 27.8 per cent of the economically

(Continued)

(Continued)

active population (Webb and Fernández-Baca, 2005, p. 535) and 52.4 per cent of the formal enterprises in Peru (PROMPYME, 2005b, p. 19). Owing to migration in the last decades, the majority of the current population of Lima comes from other cities of Peru: 36.2 per cent are direct immigrants, 43.5 per cent are second-generation immigrants, and 7.6 per cent are third-generation immigrants. Only 12.7 per cent are people from Lima whose parents were born in Lima, which is why it can be said that Lima, from the point of view of its population, represents 'all Peruvian's Peru' (Arellano and Burgos, 2004, p. 91).

Metropolitan Lima includes the province of Lima and the Constitutional Province of Callao. Peru's geopolitical structure divides it into 24 departments and a constitutional province: Callao. Each department is formed by provinces and in turn these provinces are also divided into districts. The Department of Lima is divided in 10 provinces: Barranca, Canta, Cañete, Cajatambo, Huaral, Huarochirí, Huaura, Lima, Oyón and Yauyos; and at the same time, the province of Lima is divided into 43 districts (Atlas y Geografía del Perú, Appendix I, 1999).

Chapter summary

The introduction ends with a chapter summary. This summary should not consist of more than one or two pages, in which the main aspects of this chapter are clarified.

This chapter does not include conclusions as they are not applicable.

The following example of a chapter summary is taken from Avolio's dissertation (2010):

Chapter Summary

In Peru, women entrepreneurs represent an important percentage of entrepreneurial activity; however, they are a phenomenon that has not yet been studied in depth; statistical and qualitative information is scarce, which represents a problem in understanding them and makes it difficult to develop a more favourable environment to promote their entrepreneurial activity.

This study has the purpose of identifying the profile of women entrepreneurs through the qualitative exploration of: (a) their demographic characteristics; (b) their educational, work and family backgrounds; (c) their administrative/managing abilities; (d) the nature of their enterprises; (e) the factors that have motivated them to become entrepreneurs; and (f) the principal obstacles in starting and achieving the growth of their enterprises.

The study has five purposes: (a) identify the characteristics of women entrepreneurs (demographics, education, work and family), their administrative/managing abilities and the nature of their enterprises; (b) explain the factors that have motivated women to choose entrepreneurship; (c) explain the obstacles women face in their enterprises; (d) suggest a conceptual frame to explain why women choose entrepreneurship, taking into account their backgrounds and factors that motivate them to become entrepreneurs; and (e) identify the profile of women entrepreneurs through a typology that takes into account their backgrounds and factors that motivate them to choose entrepreneurial activity.

The review of literature has made it possible to choose a conceptual model regarding women's motivations to become entrepreneurs. The model chosen is a modified version of the Orhan and Scott model (2001), considering Cooper's (1981) studies, which establish that the decision to create a new enterprise seems to be influenced by the person's background, the organizations for which the person has worked before, and the situational factors that generate a more or less favourable environment to create a new enterprise; and Goffee and Scase's (1985) typology.

The study is conducted in the area of Metropolitan Lima (Peru), considers only the formal sector of women entrepreneurs, and studies women entrepreneurs who are owners of their enterprises, and who have been involved for a minimum of two years in the formal operation of their enterprises, regardless of the way the ownership was obtained (founding, purchase or inheritance).

References

Avolio Alecchi, B. (2010). El Perfil de las Mujeres Empresarias en el Perú. [An Exploratory Study of the Profile of Women Entrepreneurs in Peru]. DBA thesis, Pontifical Catholic University of Peru.
Yin, R. (2003). *Case Study Research: Concepts and Methods*. Thousand Oaks, CA: Sage.

9 Literature review

The literature review is a very important chapter in the research paper as it demonstrates that a comprehensive review of the study subject was carried out in order to identify the gaps in the literature that justify the research. There are several texts that explain how to develop a proper literature review, such as that by J. L. Galvan (2009). These texts will provide a proper understanding of the process involved in the development of a literature review.

Initial paragraphs

As mentioned in the previous chapter, each chapter should start with a few introductory paragraphs that explain what the chapter is about. The first paragraph follows immediately after the chapter title and it should be carefully written as it is the first thing the reader will read; it must be clear and concise, and engage the reader. This paragraph should arouse curiosity in the reader so that they want to continue reading the document. These initial paragraphs are followed by the literature map. The initial paragraphs should not exceed one page.

The following example of some initial paragraphs is taken from Avolio's dissertation (2010):

> Entrepreneurship is an emerging research area among academics because it is acknowledged that fostering entrepreneurial activity is associated to a greater economic growth (Weeks and Seiler, 2001). Specifically, the interest in understanding women's entrepreneurial activity is because of the importance they are gaining in the entrepreneurial sector as well as the evidence that women encounter difficulties in starting and operating a business with are different from those faced by men. (Neider, 1987)
>
> The initial research on women entrepreneurs was focused on knowing their background and the organizational characteristics of their enterprises. The most recent studies take into consideration more extensive research studies on the problems they face, their administrative practices, the perceptions of women as entrepreneurs, their skills for success, gender differences,

role conflicts between their enterprises and their families, and the vision they have for their enterprises. Methodologically, most research studies were based on surveys and case-studies. They are mainly descriptive and use convenience samples as there are no databases of women entrepreneurs. Besides, frequently, research is not associated with any base theory. However, such studies have made it possible to obtain knowledge on which theories on women entrepreneurial activity are developing.

This chapter presents the current literature on women entrepreneurs and their enterprises. The subject has been organized from general aspects to specific aspects. In the first place, the literature on entrepreneurship in general, the growth of women entrepreneurial activity and the main results of the research studies internationally are presented. Later, research in Latin American is presented and, specifically, what is known about women entrepreneurs in Peru. Finally, the literature developed on the motives that pull these women to become entrepreneurs and the obstacles they face to start and make their entrepreneurial activity grow is examined.

Literature map

After the initial paragraphs, this chapter includes a literature map. The map reflects the relationship between the concepts and the research, as well as the corresponding authors and references. Like any map, it shows the user the different routes needed to get to their destination. In this case, the destination is the purpose of the study. The routes are the different related concepts.

There are several texts that delve into the methods needed to make a proper and comprehensive literature review. It is recommended that these are reviewed in order to develop an appropriate research paper.

The following example of a literature map is taken from Avolio's dissertation (2010):

Literature Map

The research studies done on women entrepreneurs are quite extensive in developed countries, especially in the United States, Canada and the United Kingdom, but there is not much knowledge about women and their enterprises in Latin America and, especially, in Peru. There are specific studies in France, Singapore, Russia, Ireland, Puerto Rico, China, Turkey, Hungary, South Africa, Israel, Poland, Germany, India, Lithuania, Greece and Australia.

Appendices B and C show the list of the main authors that have carried out studies on women entrepreneurs. In order to analyse the main trends

(Continued)

(Continued)

coming from these studies, the articles have been classified according to Garner's (1985) conceptual framework for the creation of new enterprises: individual, environment, organization and processes.

Most studies on women entrepreneurs have been focused on the individual. The initial studies were devoted to knowing about the background and organizational characteristics of their enterprises; most recent studies consider wider research about the problems women entrepreneurs have, their administrative practices, perceptions of women as administrators, their ability to succeed, gender differences, role conflicts between their enterprises and their families, and the vision they have for their enterprises. Methodologically, most studies are based on surveys and case studies, they are mainly descriptive and use convenience samples as there are no databases on women entrepreneurs, and they frequently do not associate research with theory. Other methodological issues are: lack of instrument validation, existence of a sole source of information, tendency to generalize behaviour and characteristics between different types of women (women that create new enterprises, women that take charge of the family business, difference of ages, industries, size) (Brush, 1992). Despite all these, such studies have produced knowledge, based on which theories on women entrepreneurial activity are being developed.

Figure 1 [Figure 9.1] shows the map of the literature and presents the main trends that have arisen from the research on women entrepreneurs and their enterprises. The individual aspects refer to the person involved in creating the new organization and include demographic aspects, background, motivations, working and educational experiences, and psychological aspects. The organization refers to the type of enterprise created; includes strategy, organizational characteristics, type of enterprise, structure and problems faced. The process refers to the actions taken by the entrepreneur to start the enterprise, and includes the identification of opportunities, search for resources, the construction of the organization, the administration of the enterprise and the response to the environment. Environment is the situation affecting and influencing the organization, and includes legal, politic, governmental, sector and technological aspects (Gartner, 1985).

Hisrich and Brush (1984) identified the typical profile of women entrepreneurs with a national survey of 468 women in the United States. They found that women entrepreneurs have similar family background, education, work experience, entrepreneurial characteristics, administrative skills and motivation; and that most women entrepreneurs were firstborns in medium class families where the father was self-employed.

Almost half of them are married with men working in professional or technical activities and have, on average, two adolescent children. Almost 70 per cent of women entrepreneurs have had basic education, and a lot of them have university degrees; their parents and husbands also have a good level of education. Most of them do not have administrative knowledge; therefore 90 per cent of them start enterprises in the service sector. Besides, typical women entrepreneurs have limited working experience, and when they do, it is in service areas like teachers, administrative positions at intermediate level or secretaries.

Their enterprises are small in terms of sales and employees. Hisrich and Fan (1991) quote a study made of 17,000 women entrepreneurs in Europe according to which more than half of them have no employees, 20 per cent employ the family and only 25 per cent employ workers that are not family members. Women entrepreneurs are individualist, creative, enthusiastic, instinctive and adaptable. In general they have the same characteristics as men entrepreneurs: they have a lot of energy, they are independent, they have confidence in themselves, and they are competitive and result-oriented (Hisrich and Fan, 1991).

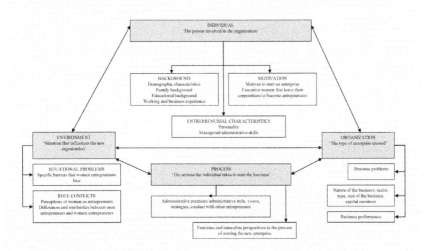

Figure 9.1 Literature map of main trends in studies on women entrepreneurs

Literature review

This is the most important section of the chapter. The literature review should be structured based on the literature map developed in the previous section. It may be worthwhile considering one subheading for each of the subjects or concepts defined in the literature map, thus making it easier to read these concepts.

Summary

This chapter includes a summary at the end. This summary should be concise and highlight the key aspects of the chapter. This section should not exceed two or three pages.

Conclusions

The literature review chapter should end with conclusions. In this case, the conclusions are very important because they identify the gaps found in previous studies and the existing knowledge in the field of study.

The conclusions should clearly express the literature gaps and they must provide an adequate justification of the purpose of the study. The conclusions should thus reflect that this purpose is an important contribution to the knowledge related to the areas that the current literature has not yet addressed.

Reference

Avolio Alecchi, B. (2010). El Perfil de las Mujeres Empresarias en el Perú. [An Exploratory Study of the Profile of Women Entrepreneurs in Peru]. DBA thesis, Pontifical Catholic University of Peru.

10 The method

The third chapter of a research paper deals with the research method. This method chapter aims to show how the study has been carried out. It includes in great detail the following aspects of the method:

a) explanation of the research design;
b) justification for the selected study design based on the theoretical elements that supported the decision to choose that design;
c) procedures used to select the cases;
d) procedures used to collect the data;
e) cases protocol;
f) presentation of the instruments, as well as the procedure for their design and development;
g) presentation of the agreed informed consent;
h) procedures for data recording;
i) procedures for data analysis and interpretation;
j) strategies to ensure the validity and reliability of data;
k) chapter summary.

This chapter always ends with a summary of the main aspects covered in the section. It has no conclusions, as this is not applicable.

Initial paragraphs

As mentioned in the previous chapters, each chapter should start with a few introductory paragraphs that explain what the chapter is about. The first of these follows immediately after the chapter title and should be carefully written as it is the first thing the reader will read; it must be clear and concise, and engage the reader. This paragraph should arouse curiosity in the reader so that they want to continue reading the document. These initial paragraphs are followed by the research design. The initial paragraphs should be no longer than one page.

The following example of the initial paragraphs in a methods chapter is taken from Avolio's dissertation (2010):

The study has exploratory purposes and it uses a qualitative approach to explore the profile of women entrepreneurs, the nature of their enterprises, the factors that stimulated them to become entrepreneurs and the main obstacles they face for entrepreneurship.

The qualitative strategy used here is multiple case studies, under a holistic design, because the research analyses women entrepreneurs. The population of women entrepreneurs comprises those women who own more than 50 per cent of a formal enterprise, who are actively involved in their operation and who generate employment for themselves and for other people, without making any distinction regarding the way the ownership was obtained. As there are no databases for women entrepreneurs in Peru, different sources have been used to identify potential participants in the study. Women entrepreneurs that have requested loans from specialized banks, information published in newspapers, referrals from personal contacts and referrals from the entrepreneurs themselves. The sample has been constructed using a combination of the following techniques: *snowball* and *maximum variation*. The cases have been rigorously chosen to reflect the diversity of situations experienced by the women entrepreneurs considering the following dimensions: age, civil status, educational level, the enterprise economic sector, the way the ownership was obtained, length of operation, and size of the enterprise. The data was collected mainly through in-depth interviews, in several sessions, in several places (mainly in their enterprises, but also in their homes or in public places), of approximately 90 minutes each. The interviews have been open, conducted by a guide. The interviews have been recorded and transcribed. Additionally, notes and photographs have been taken before starting the interviews, as well as during them, recording their comments and perceptions to capture the particular aspects of the entrepreneurs and analyse each case further. The information has been coded, categorized and analysed using analytic induction (Strauss and Corbin, 1998) and the procedures suggested by Miles and Huberman (1994) to analyse qualitative information. To process the information, the *Atlas.ti* version 5.2 software has been used.

Research design

This section explains the research design. It should specify if the purpose is exploratory, descriptive or explanatory and it should also justify with clear arguments why the research has such a purpose. Additionally, it is convenient to explain here what kind of paradigm the research will use and to justify the selection.

The following example of the information to be included in the research design is taken from Avolio's dissertation (2010):

Research Design

The study has an exploratory purpose, oriented to obtain knowledge of the factors that motivate women to become entrepreneurs, and of their relation with their demographic, educational, work and family background. The purpose is exploratory because, although there is some knowledge about women entrepreneurs, it is based mainly in developed countries. According to Hisrich and Ayse Öztürk (1999), this poses a problem in understanding women entrepreneurs, as social, familiar and work structures vary from one country to the other: 'Since the theories about women entrepreneurs have emerged primarily from research in developed countries, it is important to examine the extent to which these apply in the context of developing ones...' (p. 114). The exploratory purpose is necessary when '... the topic is new, the topic has never been addressed with certain sample or group of people, or existing theories do not apply with the particular sampling or group under study' (Creswell, 2003, p. 22).

The qualitative approach has been used in this study for the following reasons: (a) it makes it possible to capture the voice of women, 'one of the benefits of conducting a qualitative study is the freedom given to the researcher to examine the respondent's experiences more closely than it is possible in a quantitative study' (Inman, 2000, p. 80); (b) the most appropriate way of understanding the motivation of women to become entrepreneurs is to give them enough space to listen to their own stories, according to Rubin and Rubin (1995), 'through qualitative interviews you can understand experiences and reconstruct events in which you did not participate' (p. 3); (c) the qualitative approach is especially suitable for understanding the meaning of situations and actions in which the participants are involved, as well as for understanding the particular context in which participants act and the influence of context on their actions (Maxwell, 1996), as is the case of the decision taken by a woman to become an entrepreneur; (d) because 'we are still at the exploratory stage in terms of developing theories of entrepreneurship and as such, more qualitative, face-to-face methods and in-depth interviews methods are most appropriate' (Paulin, Coffey, and Spalding, 1982, quoted by Stevenson, 1990, p. 442); this is especially true about women entrepreneurs in Peru, where it is necessary to carry out preliminary work to become familiar with the phenomenon; and (e) many of the studies that have been conducted about women entrepreneurs have serious methodological limitations, basically in the design of the interviews, because the structures used to prepare questionnaires are based on male notions (Stevenson, 1990). Structured questionnaires are useful to obtain information; however, 'the best way to discover the world of women entrepreneurs is by interviewing them and letting them explain their problems' (Stevenson, 1990, p. 443).

Design justification

This section describes the strategy used in the research and explains why the design was chosen.

An example of the justification to use Yin's case study (2003) in Avolio's dissertation (2010) is shown below:

Design Justification

Yin (2003) proposed three conditions to select a research strategy: (a) the kind of questions established, (b) the degree of control that the researcher has over the events, and (c) the degree in which the events refer to current situations in contrast with historical events.

According to these conditions, the questions of this study are *what is* and *why* type of questions. Yin (2003) established the case study is the favourite strategy when the research has questions such as 'how' or 'why', when the researcher has little control over the events and when the approach is over contemporary phenomena within the context of real life (p. 1). For 'what' exploratory questions, Yin (2003) established that it is justified to conduct exploratory studies and that any of the following strategies may be used: experiments, surveys, file analysis, history or case studies (p. 6).

With regard to the degree of control over the events, the researcher must determine up to what extent the events associated to the study can be controlled. According to Yin (2003), if the researcher has the control or can manipulate the events, the best method of research may be an experiment. If the researcher has little or no control over the events, in turn, it is preferable to use a case study or a history study. In this study, the researcher has no control over the decisions of women to become entrepreneurs and the case study is preferred over other methods of research. With regards to the last condition, about the degree in which the events relate to current situations in contrast with historical events, the experiments, surveys or case studies are preferable for the first case and history for the second case. This study analyses the variables related to current entrepreneurial activity of women where context is important; therefore it is preferable to use the case study as a research method to deepen the analysis of variables, to make it possible to generate a common pattern among women entrepreneurs and establish a profile of their performance against the different factors that affect them.

Taking into account these conditions the most appropriate methodology to respond to the questions of this research is the case study. Yin (2003) established that the case study method is 'empiric enquiry that investigates a contemporary phenomenon within its real-life context, especially when the boundaries between phenomenon and context are not clearly evident' (p. 13).

Besides, the case study is an appropriate strategy for research because it makes it possible to explore women entrepreneurs in depth, in order to obtain knowledge about complex, sensitive and personal aspects, such as the decision to become an entrepreneur (Stevenson, 1990). According to Stevenson (1990):

> One becomes an entrepreneur as an evolution, through the process of encountering, assessing, and reacting to a series of experiences, situations and events. Until we know more about this process, it is inappropriate to try to measure it using structured, survey research methods. To understand the process of entrepreneurship, it is critical to understand how individual entrepreneurs attach meanings to these events and circumstances. To understand a person's motivation for starting a business, a checklist of possible motivation factors cannot capture the complexity of the decision process. Only an interview can allow full expression of the interrelationship between the many variables that can impact on one person's ultimate decision to start a business. (p. 442)

The logic of qualitative studies is inductive. Under inductive logic, the researcher obtains information from participants through the interviews and detailed observation of the largest amount of events possible, analyses the information and converts it in topics or categories. Within these categories, the researcher looks for behavioural patterns, generalizations or theories that are then compared with the literature and with past experiences (Creswell, 2003, p. 132). However, according to Ragin (1987), the case study is at the same time an inductive and a deductive process. It is deductive because it starts from a theoretical perspective that works as a guide to collect the information systematically and from analysis. It is also inductive because, after performing a transversal analysis of the cases, the patterns immersed in the information are compared.

The research has used the multiple case study strategy under a holistic approach. The case study has had a holistic design because it implies a sole unit for the analysis: women entrepreneurs. Multiple case studies are appropriate as 'the evidence from multiple cases is often considered more compelling, and the overall study is therefore regarded as being more robust' (Herriott and Firestone, 1983, as cited by Yin, 2003, p. 46). Beside, multiple cases make it possible to (a) predict similar results (literal replication), or (b) predict contrasting results, but due to predictable reasons (theoretical replication) (Yin, 2003).

Research questions

Although the research questions are presented in the introduction chapter, they may also be included in the method chapter.

The following example of the research questions is taken from Avolio's dissertation (2010):

Research Questions

The research question for the study is: What is the profile of women entrepreneurs in Peru?

The study is a qualitative exploration of the profile of women entrepreneurs in Peru, in which we try to determine the following: (a) the
demographic characteristics of women entrepreneurs; (b) the educational,
work and family background of women entrepreneurs; (c) the adminis-
trative/managing skills of women entrepreneurs; (d) the characteristics of
enterprises owned in 50 per cent or more by women; (e) the factors that
have motivated women to become entrepreneurs; and (f)e the principal
obstacles to start and develop an enterprise owned by women.

Case selection

The procedure to select the cases implies explaining the following:

a) type of sampling;
b) the method chosen to select the cases included in the sample;
c) the classification questions used to select the sample;
d) strategies to develop the sample;
e) privacy of the cases;
f) criterion for the required number of cases.

It is very important to clearly and accurately present this information, as the
procedures applied to select the cases are very important for the validity and reliability of the study.

The following example of the information to be included in the case selection
is taken from Avolio's dissertation (2010). Appendix 10.A includes an example of
the classification questions, also taken from Avolio's dissertation (2010).

Case Selection

Yin (2003) suggested three principles for data collection in case studies:
(a) using multiple sources of information; (b) creating a database; and
(c) keeping a chain of evidence in the analysis, showing explicitly the
relations between research questions, the information obtained and the conclusions (pp. 97–105). The procedures used in data collection according to
the suggestions given by Yin (2003): sources of evidence, case protocol,
pilot cases, and outline of the interviews, are described below.

Sampling

Qualitative studies do not use probability sampling or convenience sampling. They are based on a purposeful sampling, which is 'a strategy in which particular settings, persons or events are selected deliberately in order to provide important information that can't be gotten as well from other choices' (Maxwell, 1996, p. 70). The main consideration to be taken into account for purposeful sampling is the selection of individuals '… that can provide you with the information that you need in order to answer your research questions' (Maxwell, 1996, p. 70). This study uses a purposeful sampling. According to Patton (1990, p. 169), the logic and the power of purposeful sampling are based on the selection of information-rich cases for in-depth study; information-rich cases are those cases which teach us considerably about important aspects for the purpose of the study.

The purposeful sampling chosen has the following objectives for the study: to achieve representability and identify the typical cases of women entrepreneurs; to capture the heterogeneity of the population of women entrepreneurs adequately and to make sure that the conclusions represent adequately the diverse ranges of probabilities (maximum variation sample); and to examine the cases that are critical for the theories considered or that will developed in the study (Maxwell, 1996, pp. 71–72).

What is a woman entrepreneur?

It is complicated to define the population of entrepreneurs of the study as there is no unique definition generally accepted of its meaning. The definition of entrepreneur varies from one research to the other: It may refer to small businesses (Canada), new companies (German) or self-employment (Finland). Other researchers use the terms small businesses, microenterprises and self-employment interchangeably (Russia). Under a strict definition, the entrepreneur is only the founder of his business; under a broader perspective, it could refer to owners and managers of a business, regardless of how they obtained the property (foundation, purchase or inheritance).

In this study, the term entrepreneur includes women owners and managers of their companies, regardless of how they have obtained the ownership. To operationalize the definition of entrepreneur in this study, and based on previous studies (Bennett and Dann, 2000; Inman, 2000; Lee-Gosselin and Grisé, 1990; Voeten, 2002a), the term has been divided into eight criteria that have had to have been fulfilled for the person to be included in the sample. The criteria are: (a) to have an enterprise operating formally at the time of the study, to consider only formal businesses; (b) to own 50 per cent or more of the ownership of the business (shares, voting participation or entrepreneurial

(Continued)

(Continued)

activity as an individual), regardless of the way the ownership was obtained; (c) to have more than two employees, in order to separate the study from self-employment; (d) that the businesses have been operating formally for two years or more, in order to separate short-term opportunities with a long-term commitment with the business; (e) to have an important administrative role in the enterprise at the time of the study; (f) to work full time in the enterprise; (g) to receive most of their income from their enterprise; and (h) to be linked with the enterprise for a minimum of two years.

Such criteria have been defined with the following objectives: (a) to separate formal businesses from informal businesses, even if they did not start in the formal sector; (b) to separate enterprises that are owned by women; (c) enterprises with two or more employees are considered to exclude self-employment, as hiring personnel is an important step in the entrepreneurial activity; (d) to separate short-term opportunities with a long-term commitment to the business; (e) to made sure that women are managing their enterprises; (f) to make sure that women have a strong commitment with their enterprises; and (g) to separate women entrepreneurs from those who do business eventually.

Specific questions have been prepared for each of these criteria, which are shown in Appendix F, and only those women who met the criteria where chosen for the study.

Strategies

Many studies have pointed out the difficulty of finding a source from which to develop a sample of women entrepreneurs. One of the main problems in the research into women entrepreneurs is the lack of a representative database (Orhan and Scott, 2001; Stevenson, 1990). In Peru, the situation is even more difficult as there is a large informal sector of women entrepreneurs, most of them related to microenterprises and self-employment, and because there is not an association of women entrepreneurs from which to build a representative sample of the population.

The sample in qualitative studies is built theoretically. This means that the choice of the informants is led by conceptual questions and not by the search of representability (Miles and Huberman, 1994). Case studies oriented to generate theories use theoretical sampling, which means that cases are chosen to obtain a replica of previous cases, to deepen the theories that are being developed inductively, to complete theoretical categories and to provide negative or contradictory examples (Eisenhardt, 1989). According to Miles and Huberman (1994), in qualitative studies:

> Sampling is investigative; we are cerebral detectives, ferreting out answers to our research questions. We observe, talk to people, and pick up artefacts and documents. That leads us to new samples of informants and

observations, new documents. At each step along the evidential trail, we are making sampling decisions to clarify the main patterns, see contrasts, identify exceptions or discrepant instances, and uncover negative instances – where the pattern does not hold. Our analytic conclusions depend deeply on the within-case sampling choices we make (p. 29).

The sample was built using a combination of the following techniques: typical cases of women entrepreneurs; snowball, 'identities cases of interest from people who know people who know what cases are information-rich' (Miles and Huberman, 1994, p. 28); and maximum variation, so that the cases chosen comprise the largest number of situations or types of evolution, according to the alternatives shown by the literature.

Diverse sources have been used to identify potential participants in the study. The typical cases of women entrepreneurs were initially obtained through the list of women entrepreneurs that had applied for a loan from banks specializing in microenterprises and small enterprises. EDYFICAR, one of the leading financial institutions specialized in microfinance in Peru, provided their database of women entrepreneurs for this study. EDYFICAR was created in 1998 by CARE, an international non-governmental non-profit organization that has worked in Peru since 1990. EDYFICAR has approximately 96,000 clients throughout Peru, a third of them in Metropolitan Lima; and approximately 55 per cent of their credits are granted to women entrepreneurs.

According to the database provided by EDYFICAR, women entrepreneurs were identified who were located in Metropolitan Lima and had received credits for amounts over US$1,000 to 31 December, 2006. One thousand and one women entrepreneurs were identified. From this list, women whose enterprises had more than two years of operation, and had two or more employees, were selected, totalling 151 cases. From these cases, 29 women were eliminated as they did not have telephone contact data and 122 cases of women entrepreneurs were established. Thirty-two women were added to this group, who were identified through information published in the newspapers, referrals from personal contacts and referrals from the entrepreneurs themselves. All the women that were accepted to participate in the study completed the interviews entirely.

The interviews were carried out between May and December 2007. Women entrepreneurs with businesses in different economic sectors were considered, with different sizes of enterprises and different ways of access to their ownership (foundation, purchase, promotion or inheritance). Serida *et al.* (2005) determined that 74 per cent of Peruvian female entrepreneurs are concentrated in the consumer sector; 8 per cent in services to companies; 14 per cent in the transformation sector; and 4 per cent in extractive

(Continued)

(Continued)

sectors. The consumer sector groups included retailing, restaurants, bars, hotels, health services, education, social services and recreational services, among others. For this study, the sector that offer services to companies comprises financial intermediation, insurance companies, real estate agencies, consultancies, professional services companies, among others. The transformation sector is related to the manufacture, storage and transportation of goods, transportation of people, construction and communications. The extractive sector comprises agriculture, forest activity, hunting, fishing and mining. Additionally, according to statistical information about small-scale productive units in Metropolitan Lima (Van Empel, 1999), data shown in Table J20, 79 per cent of the enterprises are in the trade sector; 8 per cent in the industrial sector; 10 per cent in the services sector; and 3 per cent in other activities.

Qualitative studies use small case samples, analysed in their context and in depth (Miles and Huberman, 1994). To answer the research questions adequately, 24 cases were selected, which made it possible to obtain enough information to carry out a transversal analysis of the cases and respond to the research questions. The number of cases was selected based on the theoretical saturation; that is, the point where incremental learning from the following case is minimal because researchers do not obtain any additional knowledge (Glaser and Strauss, 1967).

According to Yin (2003), there is no rule about the necessary number of cases, as the research follows replication logic more than statistical logic. The typical criteria about the size of the sample are irrelevant; the research must think of this decision as a reflex of the number of replies of the cases the study needs or would like to have (p. 51). Multiple case study follows replication logic, which means that 'each case must be carefully selected, so that it either: (a) predicts similar results (a literal replication) or (b) predicts contrasting results but for predictable reasons (a theoretical replication)' (p. 47).

Data collection procedures

This section explains in detail the procedures used to collect the survey data. The case study should consider the following:

a)   case protocol details;
b)   the use of experimental cases;
c)   the sources of evidence (documents, observation, interviews); and
d)   the interviews scheme.

The following example of the information to be included in the data collection procedures is taken from Avolio's dissertation (2010).

Data Collection Procedures

Yin (2003) suggested three principles for data collection in case studies: (a) using multiple sources of information; (b) creating a database; and (c) keeping a chain of evidence in the analysis, showing explicitly the relations between research questions, the information obtained and the conclusions (pp. 97–105). The procedures used in data collection according to the suggestions given by Yin (2003): sources of evidence, case protocol, pilot cases, and outline of the interviews, are described below.

Case Protocol

The protocol is the agenda that guides the researcher's work. Before starting the interview, each participant has received information about the purpose of the study, the main aspects that will be dealt with and an Informed Consent from.

Pilot Cases

The first two cases were uses as a pilot to test the interview guide and to adjust and change it as necessary. As a result, several questions were modified and others were included in the guide. According to Yin's recommendations (2003), pilot cases were selected by reasons of convenience and access, in order to achieve a longer relationship between the interviewees and the researcher. Pilot cases play 'the role of a laboratory for the investigations, allowing them to observe different phenomena from many different angles or to try with different approaches on a trial basis' (p. 79). The reports of pilot cases, according to Yin's recommendation, have included explicitly the improvements in the research design and field procedures.

Interviews Outline

Women were initially contacted by phone. If it was not possible to contact someone at first, three attempts were made before excluding them for the selection. It was not always easy to make the contacts to identify potential cases of women entrepreneurs. Upon establishing telephone contact, researchers identified themselves as students from Pontificia Universidad Católica del Perú and explained the purpose of the study briefly mentioning the topics intended to be developed, as well as the importance of the investigation for establishing support programmes aimed at improving women entrepreneurial activity. If the person was interested, the researcher described the study in detail and explained the need to establish an interview, trying not to affect the entrepreneur's working activity. The most convenient date and place for the interview was agreed. During the telephone contact, classification questions were made to establish if

(Continued)

(Continued)

the person complied with the criteria of the definition of *entrepreneur*. In several cases it was not possible to establish the classification criteria clearly and it was necessary to formulate the questions that corresponded to the personal interview. Three cases were discarded at the beginning of the personal interview because they did not comply with classification questions. However, as they had already been visited, a cordial conversation was started with these women to understand the problems of a woman entrepreneur in depth. Such cases were not valid, but they made it possible to widen the criteria for the research.

The objective of the interviews was to capture the motivations of the women and the problems in their businesses. Therefore it was essential to generate trust and a sense of cooperation for the interviewees to disclose the required information. The interviews were carried out according to the case protocol. The process of the interview should be relaxed and make the entrepreneurs feel comfortable. For this purpose, they were requested to suggest the most convenient place and time for them. Most of the interviews were carried out in their work places or in their homes. Some women chose to be interviewed in their work places at midday, during their lunch time, when they had more available time and while their collaborators were resting. Others preferred to be interviewed on a Sunday morning, a Saturday afternoon, or during a weekday, so as not to interrupt their working schedule. Several interviews were carried out in multiple sessions, with an average time of two hours for the first interview and one hour for the second. The second interview was aimed at deepening and specifying details that were not dealt with in the first one because of the course of the conversation.

Many women could only devote a limited time to the study and some did not trust the objective of the interview. As many perform informal activities, some thought that the purpose of the interview was to make tax verifications and that the interviewer was an officer from the tax authority in disguise. To generate trust among the interviewees, the interviewer carried some promotional information from Pontificia Universidad Católica del Perú, as well as some photographs of the research group. Even after having agreed on the interviews, their times were often changed at the request of the women. In average, to carry out each interview, the interviewers had to wait one to two hours after the agreed time before the person contacted would receive them.

At the beginning of the interview, the researcher explained the general objectives of the study, the Informed Consent, confidentiality and the procedures of the interview. The interviews were recorded with the consent of the women entrepreneurs. The interviews were carried out according to the interview guide, shown in Appendix G [Appendix 10.B].

Every person interviewed offered a unique contribution to the study, and after overcoming the initial fears, in some cases, they were all very friendly and collaborative, and interested in the opportunity to talk about their experiences as entrepreneurs. A great deal of important information was collected, including fascinating life stories. All of them generated smiles in the researchers as well as in the interviewees, and even some intimate and personal details were addressed with the entrepreneurs.

According to Eisenhardt's suggestions (1989), the process of interviews was carried out by the researcher with the support of two research assistants specially trained for the study and knowledgeable in qualitative research methods. After each interview, the research group (main researcher and two assistants) met to interchange the experiences obtained in the interviews. As the interviews continued, the interviewers became more experienced in the way the questions were asked to the women. Carrying out the study with two research assistants made it possible to increase the potential creativity of the study complementing the conclusions with the different points of view of the researchers and thus increase the reliability of the results.

Case protocol

As previously explained, the protocol is part of the data collection procedures. Each study should develop its own case protocol. The case protocol usually has four sections: The first is intended to present an overview of the study, including the background, objectives, questions, and the theoretical framework.

The second section describes the onsite data collection procedures, including the sample data, classification questions, the interview invitation method, the signing of the informed consent, the interview schedule, the review of documents and data prior to the interview, and the recording systems.

The third section of the protocol refers to the questions included in the interview guide. Finally, the fourth section sets out how to report the case, considering the general data, forms, documents, photographs, the interview transcript, the researcher's report, and the narrative of the questions answered in the guide interview.

The following example of a case protocol model is taken from Avolio's dissertation (2010):

Case Protocol

a) Study overview

   A1 Background
   A2 Objectives of the study and research questions
   A3 Theoretical framework
   A4 Role of the protocol in research

(Continued)

(Continued)

b) Field procedures

    B1 Data of women entrepreneurs to be interviewed
    B2 Classification questions
    B3 Invitation for the interview
    B4 Informed Consent
    B5 Schedule of interviews
    B6 Documents available before the interview
    B7 Recording/photographic equipment

c) Questions of the case

    C1 Interview Guide

d) Report of the case

    D1 General Information of the executed interviews
    D2 Informed Consent signed
    D3 Documents and photographs obtained during the interview
    D4 Field notes forms
    D5 Interview note forms
    D6 Interview transcription
    D7 Researcher report
    D8 Narratives on the answers to the questions in the interview guide

Instruments

This section details the instruments used for data collection. For instance, if the instrument is the interviews, the following items shall be explained in detail:

a) the interview guide design;
b) how the different questions of the interview guide are posed;
c) the theoretical basis used to develop the interview guide;
d) the structure of the interview guide.

It is important to note that in the case study, as recommended by Yin (2003, p. 74), the guide questions are directed to the researcher and not to the respondent, in order to establish the information to be collected and its justification. This characteristic is what clearly differentiates an interview guide from a survey.

    Appendix 10.B depicts an example of an interview guide taken from Avolio's dissertation (2010). The following example of an instruments section is also taken from Avolio's dissertation (2010):

Instruments

Interviews have been carried out with a guide designed to obtain knowledge about women entrepreneurs and their enterprises, which is shown in Appendix G [Appendix 10.B]. The variables included in the interview guide are the results of a deep review of the literature regarding the variables that influence entrepreneurship. The interview guide is based on ideas from studies made in Turkey (Hisrich and Ayse Öztürk, 1999), Hungary (Hisrich and Fulop, 1994), Poland (Zapalska, 1987), Singapore (Lee, 1996), the United States (Buttner and Moore, 1997; Hisrich and Brush, 1986, 1991; Hisrich and O'Brien, 1981, 1982; Inman, 2000; Neider, 1987), Canada (Lee-Gosselin and Grisé, 1990) and China (Hisrich and Fan, 1991). Although some demographic factors such as age, civil status, education and number of children cannot be manipulated to estimate the entrepreneurial activity, research shows that they play an important role in the decision to become entrepreneurs and therefore have been included as part of the variables (Mitchell, 2004).

As Yin recommends (2003, p. 74), the questions in the guide have been aimed to the researcher and not at the interviewed, in order to establish the information that has to be collected and its justification. This characteristic is what clearly differentiates an interview guide from a survey.

The questions in the guide include the information necessary to answer the research questions. As some questions are related to personal aspects of women entrepreneurs, and in those cases where it was difficult for women to reflect upon or verbalize the circumstances through which they became entrepreneurs, a technique known as *probing* was used to let them reflect upon and explain their answers. The technique consists in keeping an interview running while more details are obtained without changing the central point in the interrogation (Rubin and Rubin, 1995). Therefore, *probing* questions have been included in the interview guide so that the women may continue talking about the matter of interest, complete an idea, explain what they have said, or obtain examples or evidence of particular details.

The initial guide questions have been oriented to establish the initial contact with the interviewee, to let them share aspects of their business and establish a relation of trust with the interviewer. The interview guide in Appendix G [Appendix 10.B] establishes: (a) the information to be requested, and (b) the questions.

The interview guide was developed based on the research questions and has nine parts: (a) general information of the interview, (b) demographic information; (c) educational background; (d) work background; (e) administrative and

(Continued)

(Continued)

managerial skills; (f) family background; (g) the nature of their businesses; (h) motives to become entrepreneurs; and (i) obstacles to starting and making their enterprises grown. The first part of the interview considers the general information of the interview. Sections (b), (c), (d), (e), and (f) have been designed to find out the background of the women entrepreneurs. Even though these factors may not be modified, the study analyses the circumstances in which the women became entrepreneurs. In this sense, this study explores the educational, work and family backgrounds as well as the administrative and managerial skills and their relation with the motivation of women to become entrepreneurs. Section (g) has been designed to find out the characteristics of businesses that at mostly owned by women. Section (h) tries to determine the reasons why women became entrepreneurs. Section (i) has been designed to understand the obstacles faced by women entrepreneurs to start their businesses and to achieve the growth of their enterprises, in order to discover the factors that may help increase the economic activity of women as entrepreneurs.

At the end of the interview, the woman entrepreneur was questioned about the possibility of contacting her again in order to clarify some aspect of the interview or with reference to other women entrepreneurs that may take part in the research.

Informed consent

The informed consent is part of the data collection process and is an important part of the protocol. In this form, the participant agrees to participate in the study and signs a consent agreement in which the study conditions, the objectives, the procedures, and the collected data confidentiality guarantee are clearly explained.

The following example of an informed consent model is taken from Avolio's dissertation (2010):

I agree to take part in the study called 'A Profile of Women Entrepreneurs in Peru: An Exploratory Study', which is conducted by Beatrice Avolio under the supervision of her supervisors, Dr Khaled Whaba and Dr Fernando D'Alessio. I understand that this participation is completely voluntary. I am able to withdraw my consent at any time with no harm, and the results of such participation, what may be identified as mine, will be given back to me and deleted from the research files, or destroyed.

I have been explained the following:

The reason for the research is to study the characteristics of women entrepreneurs and their enterprises, the reason that stimulated them to become the owners of their enterprises and the variables that stimulated the participation of women in entrepreneurial activities, to obtain information that may help to improve their entrepreneurial efforts and the governmental practices to promote women as owner of a business.

No stress or uncomfortable situation is foreseen.
There is no risk.
I agree on the following procedures:

Have interviews, with a duration of approximately two hours each, in which the researcher will ask me questions related with my demographic characteristics, my work and administrative experience, the reasons to become an entrepreneur, and the obstacles I had to start my business and make it grow. I understand that I can refuse to answer such questions and I can interrupt my participation at any time.

The information I supply will be confidential and will not be published in any way that may be personally identifiable without my prior consent. A tape recorder will be used during the interview and the answers will be transcribed with a code in order to protect my identity.

The researcher will answer any additional question, in this moment or at any time during the project.

_____   _____

Name of Participant   Name of the Researcher

_____   _____

Signature of Researcher / Date   Signature of Participant / Date

Please sign both copies, keep one and give the other back to the researcher.

Data record procedures

The data record procedures include those procedures followed by the researcher in order to record the collected data in a database, taking into account the necessary protocols that allow showing the required evidence throughout a research process. The data record procedures in a case study usually include the following aspects:

a)   the use of field notes for observations;
b)   the use of field notes during the interviews, where the researcher records his own observations and reflections on the data collection process;
c)   the method to record the interviews;

d)   how the comprised database ensures the reliability of the research;
e)   procedures for the chain of evidence;
f)   software used.

The following example of data record procedures is taken from Avolio's dissertation (2010), based on Yin's case study method (2003).

Data Record Procedures

After each case, the data from the observations as well as the notes from the interviewer comments were registered. Appendix D [Figures 10.2 and 10.3] shows the Field Note Form for the observations and the Interview Note Form. The interviews were recorded and transcribed.

To increase the study reliability, a database was developed for each case, so that the evidence for the interview carried out may be directly and clearly reviewed. The database comprises the following documents: (a) general information about the interviews carried out; (b) Informed Consent Form signed by the interviewee; (c) documents related to the case and obtained during the interview; (d) photographs of the entrepreneur and her enterprise; (e) Field Notes Form (Appendix D [Figure 10.2]); (f) Interview Notes Form (Appendix D [Figure 10.3]); (g) transcriptions of the interviews; (h) the researcher report; and (i) a report of the narratives of the answers to the questions in the interview guide, with the respective quotes (suggested by Yin, 2003, p. 103–104). These documents are kept as both hard copy and digital files.

Yin (2003) suggests keeping a chain of evidence in the analysis, showing explicitly the relations between research questions, the information obtained and the conclusions, to ensure study reliability, considering that: (a) the researcher's report includes the specific references to the sources of information contained in the database; (b) the database makes it possible to identify clearly the circumstances in which the information was obtained; and (c) the information has been collected according to the protocol procedures (p. 105).

The chain of evidence in the analysis of the study is expressed through the following: (a) the date, time and place of each interview with the women entrepreneurs is documented in the general information of the interviews carried out; (b) women entrepreneurs have signed the Consent Form to express their agreement with their participation in the study; (c) whenever possible, written information was obtained about the enterprise, which has been filed in each case database; (d) photographs were taken of the entrepreneur and her enterprise to obtain greater familiarity with the circumstances of the interview; (e) notes were taken of what was observed in the interviews, which were recorded in the database through the Field Notes Form; (f) personal notes were taken during the interview, to complement the researcher's report and have been recorded in the database through the Interview Notes Form; (g) the recordings from interviews have been transcribed; (h) the report prepared by the researcher includes specific references of the interview transcription; (i) the information has been collected by the researchers according to the procedures of the protocol; and (j) the information has been processed by the Atlas software, keeping clear evidence between the narrative and the coding of the information in the process of analysis.

Field notes forms

Several methods are used to record data. In all these methods the interviews are recorded and then transcribed. The observations are recorded on different forms, on which the interviewer writes down his observations schematically. Forms can also be used to record the researcher's reflections during the interview process.

Three forms are presented as examples of what can be used for these types of recordings (Figures 10.1–10.3). The first refers to the notes taken during the interviews with experts. The second is the form for the notes taken during the observation process. The third form is used to record the researcher's reflections during the interviews.

Software for qualitative data analysis

There are several computer programs that can be used to process qualitative data. Miles and Huberman (1994) present the most widely used software. Without doubt, Atlas.ti is the most widely used software for processing qualitative data and is very simple and easy to use for data analysis.

Data analysis and interpretation

This section explains how the data will be analysed and interpreted in order to achieve the purpose of the study. As stated by Marshall and Rossman (1999): 'Data analysis is the process of bringing order, structure and meaning to the mass of collected data. It is a messy, ambiguous, time-consuming, creative, and fascinating process' (p. 150).

In qualitative approaches, the interpretation process gives meaning to the data. Unanalysed data has no inherent meaning; interpretation gives meaning to the data and presents that meaning to the reader through the written report (p. 153).

The overall strategy used to analyse the data should be included first as a general framework. It is necessary to study the various strategies based on the selected

Interviews with the experts	
General Information	
Date	
Starting time	
Finishing time	
Place of the interview	
Name	
Organization they belong to	
Address	
Telephone	
E-mail	
Main Topics Discussed	Information Provided
Signature of Researcher	

Figure 10.1 Interview with experts form

Field Notes Form	
General Information:	
Date of the observation	
Starting time	
Finishing time	
Place of the interview	
Woman's name	
Name of the enterprise	
Name of the researcher	

Descriptive Notes	Researcher Commentaries
1 Record everything they can remember from the observation 2 Picture of the interviewee 2 Description of physical environment, structure of the scene 3 Particular events 4 Sequence and duration of events and conversations	Personal commentaries of the researcher such as ideas, impressions and prejudices (Creswell, 2003, p. 189) Record of feelings, interpretations, intuitions, preconceptions, and future areas of research (Taylor & Bogdan, 1984, p. 83)
Signature of Researcher	

Figure 10.2 Field notes form

Interview Notes Form	
General Information	
Date	
Starting time	
Finishing time	
Place of the interview	
Woman's name	
Name of the enterprise	
Name of the researcher	
Descriptive Notes 1 Picture of the interviewee 2 Picture of the physical environment 3 Reconstruction of dialogue 4 Particular events	Researcher Commentaries Personal commentaries of the researcher such as ideas, impressions and prejudices (Creswell, 2003, p. 189) Record of feelings, interpretations, intuition, preconceptions and future areas of research (Taylor & Bogdan, 1984, p. 83)
Signature of Researcher	

Figure 10.3 Interview notes form

method in order to identify the different strategies. This section is very important for the method. If it is unclear how the data will be analysed and what the stages and perspectives of the analysis are in each case and in the cross-sectional case analysis, the study will not be of good quality.

The example below, taken from Avolio's dissertation (2010), explains in detail the strategy and procedures used to analyse and interpret the case, based on Yin's case study method (2003). A perusal of Yin's book (2003) is recommended as a way of looking at the different possible strategies.

Data Analysis and Interpretation

The research has used as a general strategy of the analysis a descriptive framework to organize the case. 'This strategy is less preferable that the use of theoretical propositions or rival explanations but serves as an alternative when you are having difficulty making either one or the other approaches work' (Yin, 2003, p. 114). The descriptive framework used is based on research questions: (a) demographic characteristics of women entrepreneurs; (b) educational, work and family background; (c) administrative and managerial skills; (d) characteristics of women's enterprises; (e) factors that stimulated women to become entrepreneurs; and (f) obstacles to starting the enterprise and for its growth. As a specific strategy the transversal analysis of the cases has been used in order to identify their patterns and draw conclusions.

The analysis of the information started immediately after completing each case database and transcription of the interviews. The qualitative information has been coded, categorized and analysed using analytic induction (Strauss and Corbin, 1998) and the procedures suggested by Miles and Huberman (1994) to analyse qualitative information. For the analysis of the information the steps indicated by Strauss and Corbin (1998) have been followed: open coding (through the identification of concepts, their properties and dimensions), axial coding (relating categories at the level of properties and dimensions) and selective coding (through the integration and refining of the theory).

The process of analysis consisted in an interactive process of three activities: reduction of the information, presentation of the information and analysis (Miles and Huberman, 1994). The information was analysed according to the six phases suggested by Marshall and Rossman (1999): organize and prepare the information for the analysis; generate categories, topics and patterns through a thorough review of the information; code the categories and the topics, marking the quotes in the information; test the initial findings; look for alternative explanations for the information; and write the report.

(Continued)

(Continued)

Individual Case Analysis

There is no standard format to carry out the individual analysis of the cases; the process is typically performed through a detailed description of each case in order to find their common elements (Eisenhardt, 1989).

The first phase of the individual analysis of the cases was to enter the interview transcriptions in the Atlas software for the qualitative analysis, which facilitates the analysis of voluminous qualitative information and has several very useful tools to explore the complex phenomena hidden in the qualitative information. In this phase, the information was reviewed several times to get acquainted with the greatest amount of aspects possible and in this way have a general idea of the information and its full meaning. The second phase of the analysis comprised the process of information reduction, by creating quotations in the main paragraphs of the interviews that were transcribed. The third phase of the analysis was coding the information. The codes are 'tags for assigning units of meaning to the descriptive or inferential information compiled during a study' (Miles and Huberman, 1994, p. 56), which constitute the formal representation of analytic thinking. The information was coded according to a provisional initial list, according to Miles and Huberman's suggestions (1994). This initial list was created based on the research questions and the conceptual framework used in the study. Other codes were generated using the inductive approach suggested by Eisenhardt (1989) and arose from the knowledge provided by the interviewees. The initial list of codes was ordered according to the following topics: demographic, work, educational, and family backgrounds; administrative and managerial skills; characteristics of women's enterprises; motivations to become entrepreneurs; and obstacles to starting and making their businesses grow. From these categories, patterns were identified and the codes were ordered in specific topics. Based on the information, matrixes were built to identify the patterns, to make comparisons and verify trends.

To analyse the information, at the end of each week of the study the information collected was reviewed, as well as the field notes and the researcher's personal notes. The group of researchers met at the end of each week to talk about the results of the study and examine the data. Every two weeks there was a meeting with a colleague, an expert in qualitative research, to summarize the situation of the research, and discuss the topics, the concepts and the explanations arising from the study. In the final phase of the information, each interview was reread to write short summaries of them. These summaries made it possible to review the quotes that were made from the interviews and use them as examples in the research report. Using the Atlas software, quotes were selected from all the interviews for each coded category. This compilation of quotes for each code was used for showing trends, contrasts and similarities.

Transversal Case Analysis

After analysing each case, their transversal analysis was conducted according to the procedures suggested by Miles and Huberman (1994) and examining the information in different ways according to the suggestions by Eisenhardt (1989). Following Eisenhardt (1989), the cases have been analysed as follows: (a) the dimensions were defined according to research questions, such as demographic aspects, backgrounds (educational, work and family), administrative and managerial skills, motivations and obstacles; (b) the similarities and differences were examined for the cases in each of these categories to try to identify patterns and relations; (c) a couple of cases were selected and the similarities and differences between them were examined (the same procedure has been applied throughout the cases) in order to force comparisons that may generate new categories or concepts that were not foreseen.

The information has been analysed from different perspectives.

First: the demographic, work, educational and family backgrounds of women entrepreneurs; the administrative and managerial skills; and the characteristics of the businesses of women enterprises were identified. Codes were assigned for each identified background. Differences and similarities were identified in women's backgrounds, their skills and the characteristics of their enterprises; such similarities and differences made it possible to identify variations in the opportunities and the circumstances women entrepreneurs experienced according to their backgrounds. This also made it possible to identify that women can be differentiated according to the stage in their life cycle in which they decide for entrepreneurship.

Second: the factors and the circumstances that stimulated women to become entrepreneurs were identified. These factors have been grouped in categories that show the diversity of circumstances and motives that led women to become entrepreneurs.

Third: the different obstacles that women face in starting their businesses, managing them, and making them grow were identified. These obstacles have been grouped in categories that show the difficulties women entrepreneurs face and their common experiences.

Fourth: the previous perspectives have been combined, identifying how demographic, work, educational and family backgrounds of women entrepreneurs vary according to the circumstances in which women start their business and with their motivations to become entrepreneurs. The objective has been to understand to what extent the backgrounds of women entrepreneurs affect the factors that stimulate them to become entrepreneurs. This analysis has made it possible to propose a conceptual framework to explain why women choose entrepreneurship. Finally, the analysis has established a typology of women entrepreneurs according to the life cycle in which they decided for entrepreneurship and with the circumstances and the motives that stimulated them to choose entrepreneurial activity.

Validity and reliability

Four conditions related to the study design must be optimized in order to develop a high-quality study: *construct validity, internal validity, external validity*, and *reliability* (Yin, 2003, p. 19):

> *Construct validity* means 'identifying correct operational measures for the concepts being studied' (Yin, 2003, p. 34).
>
> *Internal validity* is only appropriate for explanatory and causal studies; it means 'establishing a causal relationship whereby certain conditions are believed to lead to other conditions, as distinguished from spurious relationships' (Yin, 2003, p. 34).
>
> *External validity* or generalization means 'defining the domain to which a study's findings can be generalized' (Yin, 2003, p. 37).
>
> *Reliability* means 'demonstrating that the operations of a study, such as the data collection procedures, can be repeated with the same results'. The goal of reliability is to minimize the errors and biases of the study.

Several strategies can be pursued to guarantee each of these conditions. These strategies must be clarified in this section of the document.

The following example of the validity and reliability section is taken from Avolio's dissertation (2010):

Validity and Reliability

To develop a high-quality study case, four conditions related to the design of the study have to be maximized: *construct validity, internal validity, external validity* and *reliability* (Yin, 2003, p. 19). To ensure these conditions, the strategies suggested by Yin (2003), Creswell (2003), and Maxwell (1996) have been used.

The following strategies have been used to ensure *construct validity*: (a) triangulation of the information, which has been collected from multiple sources including observations, interviews and documents (p. 36); (b) key informants have revised the draft reports of the cases studied (p. 36); (c) a chain of evidence has been kept in the analysis (p. 36); (d) the researcher's bias has been clearly specified (Creswell, 2003, p. 196); (e) quasi-statistics have been carried out to analyse the information related to a particular conclusion (Maxwell, 1996, p. 95); (f) two pilot cases have been carried out (Feng, 2005, p. 42).

Information triangulation makes it possible to compare several types and sources of information to achieve validity of the results. In this study, information triangulation was mainly achieved by: (a) comparing what was expressed by women entrepreneurs during the interviews with what was observed directly by the researcher during the visits carried out;

(b) verifying the information with written documentation obtained during the interview, as, for example, tax information, promotional information, operating licenses, bills of sale, among other documents, when applicable; and (c) comparing the information contained in the Field Notes Forms with the Interviewer Notes Forms and the researcher's report, to ensure the consistency of the answers obtained.

According to Yin (2003), the *internal validity* is only appropriate for explanatory and causal studies (p. 34). This logic is not applicable for exploratory or descriptive studies, where the objective is not to establish causal relationships. In this exploratory study, the priority is to infer events that may not be directly observed. The objective is not to establish a causal model, but to determine the characteristics of patterns emerging from the comparison of cases. To make sure that inferences are valid, the study used the *pattern matching* strategy; patterns emerging from the comparison of cases provide the bases to establish the conclusions to the research.

Respect to *external validity* establishes the domain to which a study's findings can be generalized (Yin, 2003, p. 34). According to Yin (2003), while the quantitative research is based on statistical generalizations, the case studies are based on analytic generalization. The analytic generalizations refers to the fact that multiple case studies may be considered as multiple experiments where the generalization is carried out analytically using a theory as a framework against which to compare the empiric results of the case under study. Analytical results may be considered as able to be generalized if the cases support the same theory. The analytic generalization is achieved relating the particular results with a wider theory. This study has used a conceptual framework as a guide for the collection of information and its analysis. The model adopted is a modified version of Orhan and Scott (2001) with regard to the motivations of women to become entrepreneurs. This conceptual framework has been analysed under *replication logic* in the different cases.

Four strategies have been used in the research to ensure *reliability*. First, the use of a protocol case where the field procedures are established, including similar procedures for the interviews, techniques to create an atmosphere of trust with the interviewee, observation notes forms, interview notes forms, time of the interview, etc.; mainly, the same interview guide is used for all the cases. Second, the use of a database of each case, with a standardized structure that makes it possible to transfer data and form a solid, complete and detailed source of the information collected. Third, the use of two research assistants in the collection of information, specially trained for the study and with knowledge about research qualitative methods. Fourth, the use of an external researcher, that has not been part of the study, in charge of verifying the contents and logic of the information analysis, comparing the conclusions obtained by the study with the ones the researcher considers as emerging from the information.

Chapter summary

The method chapter, like the introduction chapter, ends with a chapter summary. The summary clarifies the main aspects of the chapter and should not exceed two pages.

This chapter does not include conclusions, as they are not applicable. The following example of a chapter summary is taken from Avolio's dissertation (2010):

Chapter Summary

The study has used a qualitative approach to explore the profile of women entrepreneurs, the nature of their enterprises, to the factors that stimulated them to become entrepreneurs and the main obstacles they face for entrepreneurship.

The strategy of multiple study cases have been used under a holistic approach. The case study is an appropriate strategy for the study as it has allowed studying women entrepreneurs in depth, in order to obtain knowledge about complex, sensitive and personal aspects such as their decision to become entrepreneurs.

The word *entrepreneur* has been defined as *the woman who owns a formal enterprise (regardless of the way she obtained the ownership), is actively involved in the operation as a manager or administrator and generates employment for herself and for other people.* To operationalize the definition of *entrepreneur*, the term has been divided into eight criteria that must be fulfilled for an informant to be included in the sample.

As there are no databases of women entrepreneurs in Peru, different sources have been used to identify potential participants in the study: women entrepreneurs that have applied for a loan in banks specializing in microenterprises and small enterprises, newspapers, business organizations, and referrals from the entrepreneurs themselves. The sample has been built using a combination of *snowball* and *maximal variation* techniques. The cases have been rigorously selected to reflect the diversity of situations experienced by women entrepreneurs.

After completing the field work, the results of the cases studied have been summarized and ordered according to the research topics and the report has been organized by the transversal analysis of cases, with appropriate examples from them to avoid presenting any of them as a unique case. The information has been coded, categorized, and analysed using analytic induction (Strauss and Corbin, 1998) and the procedures suggested by Miles and Huberman (1994) to analyse qualitative information.

References

Avolio Alecchi, B. (2010). El Perfil de las Mujeres Empresarias en el Perú. [An Exploratory Study of the Profile of Women Entrepreneurs in Peru]. DBA thesis, Pontifical Catholic University of Peru.

Marshall, C. and Rossman, G. (1999). *Designing Qualitative Research*. Thousand Oaks, CA: Sage Publications.

Miles, M. and Huberman, M. (1994). *Qualitative Data Analysis: An Expanded Sourcebook*. Thousand Oaks, CA: Sage Publications.

Yin, R. (2003). *Case Study Research: Concepts and Methods*. Thousand Oaks, CA: Sage Publications.

Appendix 10.A: Example of Classification Questions

Information	Question	Sources of evidence	Alternatives
P1 Participation of the woman in the property	Is it a women-owned enterprise (50% of ownership or more)?	If it is a legal entity, verify in legal documents. If operating as an individual, verify in tax return documents or from a declaration from interviewee	Yes, to P2 No, discontinue
P2 Formal activities	Do you operate your business formally?	Expressed by the articles of incorporation, have a Consolidated Tax Record, have filed a Tax Return, have tax documents such as Bill of Sale or Invoice or have a municipal operating licence	Yes, to P3 No, discontinue
P3 Employees in the business	P3 A Do you have any employees? P3 B How many employees?	Verified by observation of the researcher and/ or declaration of the interviewee	Yes, to P3B No, discontinue Less than 2, discontinue More than 2, to P4
P4 Time of operation of the business	How long has your business been established?	Expressed by advertising material, rent documents, tax return or declaration of the interviewee	Less than 2, discontinue 2 or more years, to P5
P5 Role of the woman in the enterprise	Does the woman have a vital role in the administration of her business?	Checked by observation of the researcher	Yes, go to P6 No, discontinue
P6 Dedication to the enterprise	Do you work full time in your enterprise?	Checked by observation of the researcher, verified by declaration of the interviewee	Yes, go to P7 No, discontinue
P7 Source of main income	Is it your main source of income?	Declaration of the interviewee	Yes, go to P8 No, discontinue
P8 Time in the business	How long have you been the proprietor and conductor of the business?	Declaration of the interviewee	Less than 2 years, discontinue 2 years or more, finish the questions

Appendix 10.B: Example of Interview Guide

The interview guide was designed to obtain information about women entrepreneurs and their enterprises. In some cases, some test questions have been considered that are relevant for the study and that can provide important additional information.

For this guide, partner refers to the person that shares the property of the business with the woman; husband or partner refers to the person with which she married or her intimate partner, with whom she shares responsibilities without being married; and tutor is the person who was in charge of her education, clothing and housing while she was under age.

Part I: Demographic Information

Now we would like to start with some general questions

Information Requested	Question	
Origin of the entrepreneur	P1	Where were you born? (province, department)
Current address	P2	Where do you currently live?
Marital status	P3	What is your marital status?

Part II: Educational Background

Now we would like to ask you some questions about your education and your family's

Information Requested	Question	
Educational level of the entrepreneur	P4	What is your educational level? (the highest)
Type of education of the entrepreneur	P5	Do you have any complete or incomplete technical or university career, which?

Part III: Employment Background

Now we would like to ask you some questions about your employment background

Information Requested	Question	
Work history	P6	What is your work history?
	Probe P7	What was your first job?
	Probe P8	At what age did you start working?

(Continued)

(Continued)

Information Requested	Question	
	Probe P9	What other economic activities have you developed in the five years before you started the business?
	Probe P10	Have you ever worked in an enterprise?
Type of work experience	P11	What has mainly been your work experience?
	P12	What has been your work category?
Sector of work experience	P13	In what sectors have you basically developed your work?
Time of previous work experience	P14	How many years of work experience did you have before becoming an entrepreneur?
Work position before entrepreneurship	P15	What was your last job before becoming an entrepreneur?
	Probe P16	Why did you leave it? (explain the circumstances)
Experience related with the enterprise	P17	Have you had work experience similar to your current business?
	Probe P18	Do you think that experience helped you to create or purchase your business?
	Probe P19	How and who helped you in your decision to start your own enterprise?
Current work activity	P20	Do you have another job or work activity that offers economic income besides your business?
	Probe P21	Which?

Part IV: Administrative/Managerial Skills

Administrative/managerial skills include training and experience related to the management of enterprises: financial, accounting, tax, organizational, human resources, aspects, etc. The skills related with the products or services offered are not included.

Now we would like to ask you about your skills to manage your business

Information Requested	Question	
Financial skills	P22	How do you administer your business financially?
	Probe P23	How do you obtain capital?
	Probe P24	Do you plan your expenses with a budget?
	Probe P25	How do you notice the good performance of your economic decisions?
	Probe P26	How do you keep your accounting?

Marketing skills	P27	How do you take marketing decisions?
	Probe P28	How do you establish your sales policies?
	Probe P29	Do you create your own products?
	Probe P30	How do you establish prices?
	Probe P31	How do you carry out your promotions?
	Probe P32	How do you distribute your product?
	Probe P33	How do you differentiate your service?
Skills in operations and logistics	P34	How do you take your decisions on operations and logistics?
	Probe P35	How do you determine production amounts?
	Probe P36	Do you have a warehouse for your products and inputs?
	Probe P37	How do you control your stock and/or inventory?
	P38	Do you use some equipment for this purpose?
Skills in technology	P39	Do you use technology in your business?
	Probe P40	What technological equipment do you use?
	Probe P41	What use do you give to this technological equipment?
Skills in direction and human resources	P42	How do you make your decisions about the organization of your enterprise?
	Probe P43	How often do you make decisions for your enterprise?
	Probe P44	What is your policy to hire personnel?
Education and training received	P45	What experience or training (if any) prepared you to become an entrepreneur?
	P46	Thinking back, what training would have been useful to start or operate your business?

Part V: Family Background

Now we would like to ask you about your family background

Information Requested	*Question*	
Siblings	P47	How many brothers/sisters do you have?
	Probe P48	What is your position (first born child, etc.)?
Residence of the family	P49	Where does your family live (to understand the family economic situation)?
Members of the family in the business	P50	Are there any family members working in your business?
	Probe P51	Were your parents or tutors entrepreneurs?
Data of the father or tutor	P52	How old is your father?
	P53	What is your father's occupation? (before retiring)
	P54	What is your father's educational level?
	Probe P55	What is your father's maximum grade?
	Probe P56	Where/what did he study?
Data of the mother	P57	How old is your mother?

(Continued)

(Continued)

Information Requested	Question	
	P58	What is your mother's occupation? (before she retired)
	P59	What is your mother's educational level?
	Probe P60	What is your mother's maximum grade?
	Probe P61	Where/what did she study?
About your children	P62	Do you have children?
	Probe P63	How many children do you have?
	Probe P64	How old are your children?
	Probe P65	What is their educational level?
	Probe P66	What/where do they study?
	Probe P67	Who takes care of your children while you work?
Influence of family life	*Ask these questions if she has a partner, with or without children*	
	P68	How is your family life affected by your being an entrepreneur?
	Probe P69	How is your domestic routine?
	Probe P70	Do you have lunch or dinner out of your house, do you use domestic help or from relatives?
	P71	How does your family life influence your business?
	Probe P72	Do you work in your house to accommodate the career of your partner/husband or to be able to take care of your family?
	Probe P73	Do you limit the growth of your business to accommodate the career of your partner/ husband or to be able to take care of your family?
	P 74	Is entrepreneurial life affecting your personal or family relationships?
Data of the husband or partner	*Ask these questions if she has a partner*	
	P75	Is your partner an entrepreneur?
	Probe P76	Does he have his own enterprise?
	Probe P77	How old is your partner?
	P78	What is your partner's occupation or enterprise?
	P79	What is your partner's educational level?
	P80	What is the maximum level of education he reached?
	Probe P81	What/where did he study?
Support of the husband or partner in the business	*Ask these questions if she has a partner*	
	P82	Did your partner provide you with financial stability to start your business?

	P83	Has your husband guaranteed any loan for your business?
	P84	Does he work with you in your enterprise?
Support of the husband or a partner in taking care of the children	*Ask these questions if she has a partner and children*	
	P85	Do you share taking care of the children with your partner?
	Probe P86	How much does he share?
	Probe P87	What does your husband do with regard to children care?
Support of the husband or partner in domestic responsibility	*Ask these questions if she has a partner*	
	P88	Do you share domestic responsibilities with your partner?
	Probe P89	How much do you share?
	Probe P90	What domestic responsibilities are the concern of your husband?
Economic responsibility of the household	P91	How does domestic responsibility work in your family?
	Probe P92	Do you share domestic responsibility with your partner?
	Probe P93	How much do you share?
	Probe P94	Are you solely responsible for the economy of your family?

Part VI: Businesses of Women Entrepreneurs

Now we would like to ask you about your business

Information Requested	Question	
General information about the enterprise	P95	What is the legal name of the enterprise?
	P96	What is the address?
	P97	What year was the enterprise formally founded?
Legal form	P98	What is the business legal form?
Way of acquiring the property	P99	How did you become the owner of the enterprise?
Partners	P100	Do you share the property of your enterprise with somebody else?
	Probe P101	Are they members of your family?
Main business activity	P102	What is the main activity of your business?
	Probe P103	What products and services do you offer?
	Probe P104	What kind of person is your service directed to?
Role of the woman in the enterprise	P105	What is your position in the enterprise?

(Continued)

(Continued)

Information Requested	Question	
	P106	How many hours a day do you dedicate to your business?
Competition	P107	Do you consider you have competitors?
Employees	P108	How many full-time employees, including yourself and the members of your family, do you have in your enterprise?
	Probe P109	How many of them are women?
	Probe P110	How many of them are members of your family?
Size of the business	P111	What were your average monthly sales in the last year?
Performance of the business	P112	How have your sales developed in the last two years?
Sources of capital	P113	What were the sources of capital to start your business?
	Probe P114	What was your capital when you started your business?
	Probe P115	Have your received bank loans?
	Probe P116	Why?
Support received from relatives or contacts	P117	What kind of support do you receive from your relatives or contacts that may help you to develop your business in a better way?
	P118	Do you know any NGO or organization that may offer you support to develop your business?

Part VII: Motives to Become an Entrepreneur

Now we would like to ask you about the reasons to become an entrepreneur

Information Requested	Question	
General reasons	Probe P119	What made you decide to start your business? Did you have a special reason to be an entrepreneur?
To prove dissatisfaction with a salaried job	P120	Do you feel that in any of your previous jobs you were discriminated against because you are a woman?
	Probe P121	What were the circumstances?
	Probe P122	Were you unhappy with the male culture in the enterprises?
	Probe P123	Were you frustrated in your work activity because you did not feel you were developing?
	Probe P124	Do you consider that your remuneration was not fair?

	P125	Did this discrimination have any influence in your decision to become an entrepreneur?
To prove difficulties in finding a job	P126	Before you started your business, did you have difficulties in finding a job?
	Probe P127	Why?
	Probe P128	Lack of experience?
	Probe P129	Old age?
	Probe P130	No demand for your skills?
	Probe P131	Too many family responsibilities?
	P132	How old were your when you started your business?
	P133	If you were offered an interesting job position, would you leave your business?
	Probe P134	Why?
	P135	Are you interested in finding a job now?
	P136	If you decided to look for a job, do you think there would be demand for your skills?
	Probe P137	Why?
To prove the need for a flexible work schedule	P138	Did you become an entrepreneur to have a flexible work schedule and balance your family and work responsibilities?
	Probe 139	Why do you want a flexible schedule?
	Probe 140	Do you want to control your time?
	Probe 141	Do you have too much responsibility for your children?
	Probe 142	Are you a widow, have you divorced or had no family support?
	Probe 143	How do you administer your time?
	Probe 144	Do you think you have more or less time available for your family now than when you did not have an enterprise?
To prove insufficient income	P145	Did you start the business because of economic need and urgency?
	Probe 146	What were the circumstances?
	Probe 147	Was your husband/partner unemployed?
	Probe 148	Was your income not enough when you started the business
To prove situation of family business	P149	Did you obtain the business by family succession?
	Probe 150	Did the business belong to your family?
	Probe 151	Did you take up the business because of death or retirement of a member of your family?
Circumstantial factors: Existence of entrepreneurial models	P151	Did you have any experience in your youth that contributed to your decision to start your own business?

(Continued)

(Continued)

Information Requested	Question	
	P153	When you were younger, were your parents or any close relatives entrepreneurs?
	Probe P154	What kind of business did they have?
	Probe P155	Did you work with them?
	Probe P156	What did you do in that business?
Circumstantial factors:	P157	Was your business a family enterprise?
Existence of support for the entrepreneurial project	P158	Did you have economic or emotional support for your business?
	Probe P159	Who gave it to you?
	Probe P160	How did they help you?
	P161	How did the members of your family react when they knew about your decision to create your own enterprise?
	Probe P162	Did they help you or not?
Pull factors	P163	Have you always wanted to be an entrepreneur? (need for achievement)
	P164	Did you become an entrepreneur to achieve independence? (wish to be her own boss)
	P165	Did you become an entrepreneur to achieve status and power? (need for achievement)

Part VIII: Obstacles to Starting and Making the Enterprise Grow

Now we would like to ask you about the obstacles you face as an entrepreneur

Information Requested	Question	
Challenges as an entrepreneur	P166	What have been the greatest challenges to starting and operating your business?
Experience	P167	Did you have enough administrative experience to start your business or was it an obstacle?
Access to financing	P168	What problems did you have when you decided to ask for a loan?
	Probe P169	Did you get the money quickly?
Education	P170	Do you think that your type of education was a problem in administering your business?
Support in the management of your business	P171	Who helps you in your business decisions?
	P172	Do you belong to any business organization or association?

Part IX: Closing Questions

P182	Is there any other topic that we have not covered that was important in your experience as woman entrepreneur?
P183	Would you mind if we contact you again to clarify any topic that we discussed today?
P184	Do you know any other woman entrepreneur that would be willing to participate in the study? (name, business, telephone number)

11 Presentation and discussion of the results

This chapter, as its name implies, has two sections: (a) First, it presents the research results; (b) then, it discusses the obtained results by comparing them with previous studies and the literature review chapter. Unquestionably, this is the most important part of the document as it describes the purpose of the study; the presented results should answer clearly and directly the questions posed in Chapter 1, the introduction.

In research papers it is very important to consider both these sections. Each section is usually organized with the same number of subheadings and research questions. For each question, the results are presented (in qualitative studies) in tables showing the frequency and then these results are discussed. Students often make mistakes in this chapter, as they confuse the presentation of the results with the discussion, leading to this section being presented in a disorganized and incomprehensible way.

Initial paragraphs

As with the earlier chapters, this chapter should start with a few introductory paragraphs that explain what the chapter is about. The first of these goes immediately after the chapter title and it should be carefully written as it is the first thing the reader will read; therefore, it must be sufficiently clear and concise, and engage the reader. This paragraph should arouse curiosity in the reader and encourage them to continue reading the document. The initial paragraphs should not exceed one page and sometimes, as in the following example, one paragraph is sufficient.

The example below is the initial paragraph in Chapter 4: Presentation and discussion of the results, taken from Avolio's dissertation (2010):

> After completing the field work, the results of the cases studied have been summarized and organized according to the research questions. The report has been organized on the basis of the transversal case analysis; the information on each case is scattered throughout the report, according to the research questions. None of the cases is presented individually, and the report includes appropriate examples from the cases. The purpose of this chapter is to present and discuss the results of the research.

Profile of the informants

The first subheading of the presentation and discussion of the results chapter usually includes the informants' profile descriptive statistics. In this chapter it is appropriate to include the following items:

a) a table with an abstract of the informants' profiles;
b) an appendix with a brief narrative presentation of each case;
c) a table summarizing the informants' response rate, in which the potential informants and the ones that couldn't be reached are listed, the total database of informants, the contacted cases, the ones that did not meet the criteria, the cases that refused to participate, the refusal rate (informants that refused to participate versus the contacted cases that met the criteria), and the acceptance rate (informants who agreed versus the cases that met the criteria);
d) cases selection criteria, in order to show that the cases were selected to reflect the heterogeneity of the informants; it is important to detail the aspects applicable to the study, such as the age and education of the informant, the organization to which the informant belongs and its characteristics, etc.;
e) study cases statistics: all the pages and spaces containing the transcripts and audio of the case studies.

The following example of a profile of the informants is taken from Avolio's dissertation (2010):

Profile of the Informants

The summary of the profiles of women entrepreneurs is shown on Table 1 [Table 11.1], and Appendix K includes a brief presentation of the background of each informant. Twenty-four cases of women entrepreneurs were reviewed and this has allowed sufficient information to be obtained to answer the research questions. For confidentiality reasons, the names of the women have been modified, and pseudonyms have been used. According to the database obtained, 151 cases were selected; 29 women with no telephone data were eliminated, and 122 cases of women entrepreneurs were identified. Thirty-two women, who were identified through information published in newspapers, personal contacts referrals and referrals from the women entrepreneurs themselves, were added to this group. All women who agreed to participate in the study completed the interviews in full. Table 2 [Table 11.2] shows the response rate of informants. Considering only the persons who accepted or rejected the invitation to participate, 34 per cent of the sample accepted to participate in the study. This does not include women who were impossible to contact by phone or those who did not meet the classification criteria of the research.

(Continued)

(Continued)

Table 11.1 Profile of the informants

Name	Place of birth	Current age	Educational level	Children	Current marital status	Business sectors	How did you come to own the enterprise?	Years the enterprise has been in operation	Number of employees	Date of interview
Carmela Arequipa	Arequipa	45	Complete High School	3	Partner	Restaurant	Foundation	6	3	5/05/2007
Enit Moyabamba	Moyobamba	30	Complete Technical Education	1	Married	Hairdresser salon	Foundation	4	8	13/05/2007
Gloria Lima	Lima	47	Complete University Education	2	Married	Jewellery production and sale	Foundation	6	4	14/05/2007
Marcelina Áncash	Áncash	57	Incomplete Primary School	3	Married	Consumer products	Foundation	15	8	15/05/2007
Rosaluz Piura	Piura	42	Complete Technical Education	3	Partner	Hairdresser salon	Foundation	2	5	16/05/2007
Francisca Arequipa	Arequipa	52	Incomplete High school	5	Married	Dressmaking	Foundation	2	10	7/06/2007
Ruth Apurímac	Apurímac	51	Incomplete Technical Education	3	Married	Bakery	Foundation	15	5	20/06/2007
Margarita Lima	Lima	50	Incomplete University	2	Married	Sale of plants	Foundation	9	5	11/07/2007

Name	City	Age	Education		Marital status	Business sector	Ownership	Years	Size	Date
Gabriela Molina	Lima	44	Complete University Education	4	Married	Building	Foundation	14	45	30/08/2007
Jesusa Rímac	Lima	58	Complete Primary School	4	Married	Sale of fabrics and derivatives	Foundation	10	7	1/09/2007
Silvia Lima	Lima	20	Incomplete Technical Education	0	Single	Textile design and print	Heritage	6	11	6/09/2007
Bety Lima	Lima.	37	Complete Technical	3	Married	Education	Foundation	4	10	7/09/2007
Teresa San Borja	Arequipa	40	Complete University Education	0	Single	Early childhood education	Foundation	14	15	18/09(2007
Mónica Surco	Lima	40	Complete Technical Education	2	Married	Hairdresser salon	Purchase	5	18	27/09/2007
Liliana Piccolo	Italia	71	Complete Technical Education	2	Widow	Pizza parlour	Foundation	29	20	4/10/2007
Liliana Minera	Lima	40	Complete Technical Education	2	Married	Sale of Machine replacements	Foundation	12	14	9/10/2007

The cases have been rigorously selected to reflect the heterogeneity of the women entrepreneurs. The cases included reflect the following dimensions: (a) the age of the women entrepreneurs, in order to reflect the different stages of the life cycle when women start the entrepreneurial activity; (b) the educational level of the woman, in order to reflect the different socioeconomic levels of the women; (c) the business sector of the enterprise, in order to show the diversity of economic sectors women entrepreneurs participate in; (d) the way how she came to own the enterprise (foundation, purchase from a third party, family succession, purchase from a relative, promotion or incorporation to the enterprise by the owners); (e) years of operation of the enterprise; and (f) size of the enterprise (estimated through the number of employees).

(Continued)

(Continued)

Table 11.2 Informants' rate of response

	Number of women entrepreneurs
Potential informants on data base	151
Other potential informants	32
Not possible to contact (no telephone)	(29)
Total base of informants	154
Women contacted	90
Women who did not fulfil the criteria	20
Women who did not accept the study	46
Women who accepted	24
Rejection rate (did not accept / women contacted who met the criteria)	66%
Acceptance rate (accepted / women contacted who met the criteria)	34%

Presentation and discussion of the results

This section aims to present the results and then discuss them. It is important to keep in mind that the following information should be included in this section:

The first thing is to explain how the information has been analysed and what the analysis perspectives are. This explanation must be consistent and similar to the information included in the research method chapter, in the data analysis section.

This section is organized according to the research questions. It will have as many subheadings as there are study research questions. If the study has five research questions, then there will be five subheadings, each one aimed to present and discuss the results related to these questions.

Presentation of the results should include the obtained data in properly formatted tables in order to reflect the results of the study. The quantitative data are presented in a narrative summary and in tables, while qualitative data are presented in narrative and in matrices.

Discussion of the results should include written analytical comments on the presented data, comparing the results with the conclusions of the previous studies given in the literature review chapter. It is important to note that the results discussion is not about repeating the information included in the tables, but to analyse the information.

Finally, verbatim quotes are included in qualitative studies. This means that the informants' quotes, that are relevant as examples of the results, are included. It is not necessary to include many quotes, one or two are sufficient. These quotes must be properly referenced, so that they can be identified in the software that enabled immediate processing of the information, thus achieving the necessary chain of evidence to confirm the study reliability. The quotes usually indicate the name of the case, according to the name included in the software, and the lines where the quote is located in the interview transcription.

The following example of the presentation and discussion of the results is taken from Avolio's dissertation (2010):

Presentation and Discussion of the Results

The results of the study are presented according to the research questions. The quantitative information is presented in a narrative summary and in tables, while the qualitative information is presented in narrative form and in matrices.

The information has been analysed from four perspectives.

First: The differences and similarities in demographic, work, educational and family background of women entrepreneurs, in administrative and management skills, and in the characteristics of women-owned enterprises have been identified, which made it possible to identify variations in opportunities and circumstances experienced by the women according to their background. The results have enabled the common patterns in the background of women entrepreneurs to be identified, as well as recognizing that women can be differentiated according to the stage of their life cycle when they decided to become entrepreneurs.

Second: The factors that influenced women to decide on becoming entrepreneurs have been identified. The analysis has identified two categories of factors: (a) circumstances and (b) motives.

Third: The diverse obstacles that women face in starting, managing and making their enterprises grow have been identified, which reflects the common experiences women face in their enterprises. The analysis has identified two categories of obstacles: (a) those related to the gender of the entrepreneur, and (b) those common to the entrepreneurial activity and not related to gender.

Fourth: The previous perspectives have been combined, and how the demographic, work, education and family background of women entrepreneurs differs according to the circumstances they initiate their enterprises in, and their motives to become entrepreneurs, have been identified. The goal has been to understand up to what point the background of women entrepreneurs affects the factors that have motivated them to become entrepreneurs. This analysis has made it possible to propose a conceptual framework to explain why women choose entrepreneurship. Finally, the

(Continued)

(Continued)

analysis has enabled a typology of women entrepreneurs to be established, according to the phase of the life cycle when they decided to become entrepreneurs, and the circumstances and motives that have stimulated them to choose entrepreneurship.

Factors in Becoming Entrepreneurs

Women are influenced by a series of factors when it comes to their decisions to become entrepreneurs; these factors have been identified in the study from the discourse of the informants and have been compared with previous literature.

The factors that arose from this investigation with regards to the decision of the women to become entrepreneurs have been grouped into two categories: circumstances and motives, to differentiate those factors of extrinsic origin from those of intrinsic origin to the women entrepreneurs. The motives identified in previous literature do not make a clear difference between circumstances and the personal motives that influence women to choose entrepreneurship.

The circumstances identified refer to events or situations that, in a set context, motivated these women to become entrepreneurs. These circumstances can be objective happenings (such as the death of the father in a family enterprise or the loss of a dependent job) or situations that influence entrepreneurship according to the woman's perception (such as dissatisfaction with the family income or the lack of prospects for professional growth).

The results of the study show that women are influenced to choose entrepreneurship by economic, work, family and personal circumstances. Economic circumstances are: economic needs or dissatisfaction with the family income. Work circumstances are: difficulty in finding a job as the lack of skills restricts the opportunities in the work market; old age or lack of education; lack of prospects for professional growth; frustration with work for economic reasons; or considering entrepreneurship as the logic continuation of professional growth. Family circumstances are: when entrepreneurship is the way to play their family role and by voluntary family succession, either by opportunity or need. Personal circumstances are: an entrepreneur role model who serves as a reference for the woman; relatives who motivate and support entrepreneurship; personal dissatisfaction; or a specific opportunity.

Motives are defined as 'the construct that represents a force in the brain that organizes perception, understanding and behavior in such a way that it changes a dissatisfactory situation and increases satisfaction' (Murray, 1938, p. 24). The motives expressed by the women in their decision to become entrepreneurs are related to achievement, autonomy, power and affiliation.

The origins of circumstances influencing entrepreneurship are extrinsic to the woman and are related to external situations that can influence them in a positive or negative way towards entrepreneurship; while the origins of motives that influence entrepreneurship are intrinsic to the woman. The motives tend to persist in time, while circumstances are modified according to the women's experiences.

There is rarely a sole circumstance or a single motive influencing a woman's decision to choose the entrepreneurial activity. Entrepreneurship results from a combination of several circumstances or motives; that is, the factors cannot be considered as mutually excluding and the same person can be influenced by many circumstances and many motives at the same time. Table 36 [Table 11.3] shows the conceptualization of the circumstances and motives identified in the study, and Tables 37 and 38 [Tables 11.4 and 11.5] show the matrix of circumstances and motives identified in each case. The cases analysed have been categorized according to the circumstances and the motives that have arisen from the study. Results show the diverse patterns existing in terms of factors that have motivated women to become entrepreneurs. Each case can be categorized into several circumstances and motives, which is why the number of total cases is higher than the number of women informants.

Thirteen women informants expressed through their discourse that their decision to choose entrepreneurship was influenced by economic circumstances: eight of them for basic economic needs; while the other five, for dissatisfaction with the family or personal income.

Nine women informants attributed their decision to work circumstances: two of them because of the difficulty to find a job; four because of lack of prospects for professional growth in their dependent jobs; three of them because of frustration with work, for feeling inadequately paid with regards to their economic expectative; and one of them because she considered entrepreneurship as the continuation of her professional growth.

Six women informants referred to family circumstances: one of them owing to the need of taking over the family enterprise because her father was ill; one of them for voluntary family succession; and five of them because the enterprise was a way to play their roles of mothers and partners, generating jobs for the family and granting safety to its members.

There were personal circumstances present in all the informants; 22 of them reported having been influenced by an entrepreneur role model and 22 said they had people close to them who supported them and motivated their entrepreneurial initiative; two women said they chose entrepreneurship because of personal dissatisfaction, and three of them, because of a specific opportunity.

(Continued)

(Continued)

Table 11.3 Identified circumstances and motives in women entrepreneurs

Circumstance	Definition
Economic: basic economic need	When the woman is the only or principal responsible for the family economy and has no other alternative than to become an entrepreneur to sustain the family. The woman created her enterprise only to gain money. Having the principal or sole economic responsibility in the household makes the woman turn to the entrepreneurial activity to obtain income.
Economic: dissatisfaction with the family income	When the woman chooses to become an entrepreneur because the family income is not enough to generate savings, develop economically, give better opportunities to their children, have funds for entertainment and give better quality of life to the woman and her family, even if such income can cover the basic household expenses.
Work: difficulty in finding a job because of lack of opportunities in the labour market	When the woman chooses entrepreneurship because of a lack of opportunities in the work market. This lack of opportunities is not related to the skills, age or education of the woman, but to external aspects such as the economic or political situation.
Work: difficulty in finding a job because of lack of skills	When the woman tries to find a job does not succeed as she lacks skills with regards to the demand on the labour market.
Work: difficulty in finding a job because of old age	When the woman tries to find a job but does not manage to because of her age and there is no demand for people her age.
Work: difficulty in finding a job because of insufficient education	When the woman tries to find a job but does not manage to for lack of adequate training with regards to the demand in the labour market.
Work: lack of perspectives of professional growth	When the woman has little chance of being promoted in a dependent job, and this generates a personal frustration.

Work: frustration for economic reasons	When the woman considers she is being inadequately paid in a dependent job and this generates a personal frustration.
Work: dissatisfied with a male culture	When the woman is dissatisfied with the existence of a male culture in her work environment, so she is not offered the same conditions as men.
Work: logical continuation of professional growth	The circumstance refers to women who have a dependent work experience and consider entrepreneurship as the logic next step in their professional growth.
Family: role of the woman in the family	When the entrepreneurial activity is closely linked to the role of mother and woman in the family; the enterprise is seen as a way of fulfilling the role of mother, through the generation of work positions for the children and the husband/partner, an independent source of income, and more security for the members of the family.
Family: voluntary family succession	The woman enters the entrepreneurial environment following a family succession line: the father/mother/tutor gives her the possibility of working and directing the family enterprise and maintaining the continuity of the enterprise in time. Family succession is voluntary when the woman entrepreneur has the initiative because she wants to work in the family enterprise.
Family: family succession by opportunity	When the family succession happens because the relative invites the woman to be a part of the enterprise; entrepreneurship arises as a work opportunity in the family enterprise.
Family: forced family succession	When the family succession happens because some family circumstance forces the woman to join the family enterprise. Entrepreneurship happens as a result of the obligation to play a role inside the family.
Family: need for a flexible schedule	The circumstance refers to the woman's requirement of a work schedule that allows her to combine her responsibilities at work with those of the household and child care.
Personal: presence of an entrepreneur role model	When the woman has an entrepreneurship reference role model, who provides knowledge, motivation, support or courage.

(Continued)

(Continued)

Circumstance	Definition
Personal: relatives who motivate and support entrepreneurship	When the woman entrepreneur has people close to her personal life (parents / tutors / relatives / friends / acquaintances / partner / husband) that motivate her towards entrepreneurship. They can be: parents who motivate the personal and professional development of their children through better educational levels and access to opportunities; role models who represent examples of work and achievement; partners that promote entrepreneurship, etc.
Personal: personal dissatisfaction	When the woman chooses entrepreneurship to "have something important to do", when her economic needs are covered and the enterprise is a source of personal satisfaction rather than income.
Personal: specific opportunity	When the woman chooses entrepreneurship for some specific opportunity, as for example, the opportunity to acquire the enterprise she works in.
Motive of *achievement*	Related to carrying out a task that has a certain degree of difficulty, and that needs to be developed swiftly and independently, besides surpassing obstacles and reaching a level of excellence (Murray, 1938, p. 164). This need to reach excellence motivates surpassing obstacles, striving to do difficult things as well and fast as possible (Murray, 1938).
Motive of *autonomy*	Related with the desire to be independent and act according to her own will, without being subject to pressure or coercion exerted by an authority or by others in general (Murray, 1938).
Motive of *affiliation*	The motive of affiliation implies the need to establish cooperation and reciprocity links, as well as the wish to gain the affections of a significant person (Murray, 1938).
Motive of *power*	The motive of power is the need to control others' feelings and behaviour; the wish to exert influence over others using suggestion, seduction, persuasion or commands; it consists in persuading others to act according to one's wishes or needs (Murray, 1938, p. 152).

The patterns identified with regards to personal circumstances show that two factors have an important influence on stimulating entrepreneurial activity: (a) the existence of people who motivate and support entrepreneurship; and (b) the presence of an entrepreneur role model. These factors have not been clearly considered in previous literature. In the first case, they are people close to the women, who motivate them towards entrepreneurship, help them in their personal and professional development, allow them access to opportunities and act as role models that represent examples of work and achievement. Results show that this circumstance is found in most women entrepreneurs: the women mention having people close to them who motivated them towards entrepreneurship, a father figure or a partner who promoted the formation of the enterprise. This kind of support has a very important component of emotional support; that is, the presence of some relative, friend or acquaintance that motivated her and encouraged her to create the enterprise. In most cases, this role is assumed by the parents or husband/partner of the woman entrepreneur. The entrepreneur role model, in turn, plays the role of reference for the woman, constitutes a source of knowledge on entrepreneurial activity and an example for the women to emulate or use as experience before creating their enterprises. The entrepreneur role model is an example of entrepreneurial activity for the woman, gives her courage to decide to become an entrepreneur and allows her to access the knowledge needed to develop entrepreneurial activity.

With regards to the motives identified in the study, all informants have expressed *achievement* and *autonomy*, while few of them have expressed *affiliation* and *power*. These results are not consistent with what was found in Singapore by Lee (1996), who pointed out that women were motivated by a high need of achievement and power, while the *autonomy* and *affiliation* motives were moderate.

Twenty-three informants have expressed *achievement* through their discourse, as: (a) need to 'reach a dream' they have always had; (b) high capacity of work and personal effort to keep the entrepreneurial project going; (c) the passion they show for their entrepreneurial activity; (d) their active pursuit of success in their entrepreneurial activities; (e) their attitude oriented to taking on challenges and seizing opportunities; (g) their attitude oriented to a high level of commitment and perfection in their activities, that is, the intention to assume more responsibilities than those directly entrusted, in order to distinguish themselves from the rest of people and to try to 'do things better than the rest'; (h) their high motivation to learn, an expression of curiosity that puts them in a situation of continuous learning; and (i) their intention to achieve economic success, as the development opportunities entrepreneurship offers are unlimited.

(Continued)

(Continued)

Eighteen out of the 24 informants expressed *autonomy* through: (a) their desire to be 'their own boss'; (b) the need to reach economic independence from their husbands/partners or family, which generates a self-value that fills them with pride and satisfaction; (c) the need to control their own lives; (d) the need to have something on their own they can control and through which they can express themselves; and (e) the need to be autonomous in their decisions and not having to wait for other people to approve their decisions.

Seven women entrepreneurs expressed *affiliation* through their desire of obtaining social value by earning the esteem of an important group, mainly their family. Three women entrepreneurs expressed *power* through their desire for status and directing other people's activities.

The literature shows a wide range of possible motivations for women. In Asia and Latin America, Kantis *et al.* (2002) found as factors the need for achievement and personal development, and the desire to be their own bosses. The factors found in the United States are related to the need for achievement, the need for independence, the need for greater work satisfaction, economic needs, the higher possibility of combining their responsibilities at home with their work responsibilities, frustration with work, unemployment, boredom or widowhood, opportunity, status, power and work security, the opportunity to undertake challenges, self-determination and the need to balance family and work responsibilities (Brush, 1992; Buttner and Moore, 1997; Goffee and Scase, 1985; Hisrich and Brush, 1986; Schwartz, 1976). In Canada, the factors identified include: an old dream, the desire to use their own talents, acknowledgement from others, logical continuation of the work experience, need to control their own lives, need to keep updated, the use of their own talents, economic need, have something on their own, to have something they can control and through which they can express themselves, creating job positions for the family, and having a better quality of life because the job is too demanding and limiting to motherhood (Lee-Gosselin and Grisé, 1990). In South Africa, the factors identified include the need for independence, need for material incentives, need for achievement, need to keep learning and the need to gain more money to survive (Mitchell, 2004).

Previous literature frequently explains women entrepreneurs' motives to start their enterprises through the *push* and *pull* factors (Buttner and Moore, 1997) and the family environment (Orhan and Scott, 2001). The *push* factors are related to needs that prevent the individuals from taking a different alternative to self-employment, such as insufficient family income, dissatisfaction in paid jobs, difficulty in finding work and need for a flexible schedule.

The *pull* factors refer to self-fulfilment, independence with regards to a hierarchical structure or the wish for status (Orhan and Scott, 2001). The *push* factors are more related to the negative circumstances that lead to entrepreneurship, and the *pull* factors to internal positive motives or needs that drive entrepreneurial activity. However, the *push/pull* model does not clearly distinguish external circumstances or situations from personal motives, and assumes the *push* factors have a negative connotation.

The literature makes no clear difference between women's motives and circumstances in becoming entrepreneurs. The results are consistent with many of the motives found in the literature explaining the factors that influence entrepreneurship. According to the literature, the need for a flexible schedule to tend to the family responsibilities is a very powerful motive for women to become entrepreneurs, as is the existence of a masculine culture in the work environment (Minniti *et al.*, 2005; Orhan and Scott, 2001). However, the results of the study show that the need for a flexible schedule and the existence of a male culture in the work environment are not motives that have stimulated women to become entrepreneurs. The results do not reinforce what the literature indicates, as in many cases women face more complicated schedules than those in dependent jobs, and because of that, this motive does not acquire much importance. With regards to masculine culture in the work environment, the results show that women do not perceive this situation or that they evaluate it differently than is shown in the literature (Carter and Cannon, 1992). None of them declared feeling that a masculine culture in the work environment impeded them from reaching any work position. On the contrary, they consider that the masculine culture is another challenge to prove their work capability. When referring to situations where they had to face a masculine culture, the women answer by describing the ways in which they were able to overcome such barriers. This does not mean that the masculine culture has not prevented them from reaching a better position in a dependent job, but shows these women do not perceive it that way.

The circumstances found in the study are explained in detail next. Results show that women entrepreneurs have experienced the following circumstances with regards to their decisions to become entrepreneurs (Table 37) [Table 11.4]):

Basic economic need. This circumstance includes those women who did not have another choice and saw themselves needing to start an enterprise just to make money. There is no doubt there are economic incentives in any entrepreneurial initiative that allow the owner to satisfy their needs, but this circumstance makes reference to the situation where the economic responsibilities of the woman (sole or principal in the household) are the main circumstance that motives her to create an enterprise, and she does not have any other alternative to support her family. As opposed to the *dissatisfaction with the family income* motive, the enterprise is approached as the way of basic support of the woman and her family. Eight women presented the *basic economic needs* motive to choose entrepreneurship, as is the case of Vilma Mundo and Rosaluz Piura:

(Continued)

(Continued)

Table 11.4 Matrix of circumstances and motives that influenced the decision of becoming entrepreneurs

Circumstances and motives	Vilma Mundo	Marcelina Áncash	Cecilia Moy	Edna Marsano	Bety Lima	Margarita Lima	Lorena Boston	Lidia Puno	Rosa Santa María	Miriam Médicis	Doris España	Francisca Arequipa	Rosaluz Piura	Liliana Minera	Carmela Arequipa	Gloria Lima	Teresa San Borja	Mónica Surco	Liliana Piccolo	Silvia Lima	Ruth Apurímac	Jesusa Rímac	Gabriela Molina	Enit Moyobamba
EC Basic economic need	X	X		X		X		X					X		X	X						X		X
EC Dissatisfaction with family income				X	X	X				X					X	X					X	X		X
FC Forced family succession																				X	X			
FC Voluntary family succession				X			X												X	X	X			
FC Role of the woman in the family						X														X	X			
WC Difficulty in finding a job for lack of work opportunities, demand for her skills, old age or insufficient education																	X							
WC Lack of perspectives of professional growth			X		X									X									X	
WC Frustration with work for economic reasons												X										X		X
WC Logic continuation of professional growth																								
PC Personal dissatisfaction																X	X	X	X	X	X	X	X	X
PC Specific opportunity	X			X	X	X	X	X	X	X	X	X	X	X	X	X	X	X	X	X	X	X	X	X
PC People who motivates and supports entrepreneurship		X	X	X	X	X	X	X	X	X	X	X	X	X	X	X	X	X	X	X	X	X	X	X
PC Presence of entrepreneur role model	X	X	X	X	X	X	X	X	X	X	X	X	X	X	X	X	X	X	X	X	X	X	X	X

PM AFFILIATION Social value								X								X	X	X
PM AUTONOMY Wish to be her own boss	X					X			X		X	X	X		X	X		X
PM AUTONOMY Economic autonomy with regard to partner or family		X		X										X				
PM AUTONOMY Need to control their own lives		X	X		X	X			X		X				X		X	
PM AUTONOMY To have something they can control and allow them to express themselves	X	X		X	X		X				X	X						
PM AUTONOMY Autonomous decision-making		X		X	X						X		X		X		X	
PM ACHIEVEMENT Driven to reaching a dream	X	X		X					X		X							
PM ACHIEVEMENT Work and personal effort capacity	X	X	X	X	X	X	X	X	X	X	X	X	X	X	X	X	X	X
PM ACHIEVEMENT Passionate about what they do	X	X		X		X	X		X	X					X		X	
PM ACHIEVEMENT Active search for success	X	X	X	X	X	X	X	X	X	X	X	X	X	X	X	X	X	X
PM ACHIEVEMENT Permanent wish for improvement	X	X	X	X		X	X						X					X
PM ACHIEVEMENT Capable of undertaking challenges	X	X	X	X	X	X	X	X	X	X	X	X	X	X		X	X	X
PM ACHIEVEMENT Do things better than the rest	X	X		X	X	X		X							X	X		X
PM ACHIEVEMENT High motivation to learn	X		X		X		X				X					X		X
PM ACHIEVEMENT Achieve economic success		X													X	X	X	X
PM POWER		X	X								X							

(Continued)

(Continued)

Table 11.5 Analysis of cases of women entrepreneurs

Case	Economic	Work	Family	Personal	Motive of achievement	Motive of autonomy	Motive of affiliation	Motive of power
Silvia Lima			X					X
Teresa San Borja		X		X	X	X		
Rosa Santa María				X	X	X		
Vilma Mundo	X			X	X		X	
Enit Moyobamba		X		X	X	X		
Francisca Arequipa		X		X	X	X		
Cecilia Moy		X		X	X			
Gabriela Molina	X	X		X	X	X		
Liliana Minera		X		X	X	X	X	
Doris España				X	X		X	
Bety Lima	X	X		X	X	X	X	

Mónica Surco				X	X	X		
Miriam	X			X	X	X		X
Médicis								
Edna Marsano	X		X	X	X	X	X	
Lidia Puno	X			X	X	X		
Gloria Lima	X		X	X	X	X	X	
Lorena Boston				X	X	X	X	
Rosaluz Piura	X			X	X	X	X	
Margarita	X			X	X	X		
Lima			X					
Marcelina	X			X	X	X		
Áncash								
Ruth Apurímac	X		X	X	X	X		X
Carmela	X			X	X	X		
Arequipa								
Liliana Piccolo	X	X	X	X	X	X		
Jesusa Rímac	X	X	X	X	X	X		
Total	13	9	6	24	23	18	7	3

(Continued)

(Continued)

Why did you decide to start your enterprise? Because I had to fight hunger and poverty. That was my mission and my task. And I have had to do it, and I've done it with effort.

(Vilma Mundo 107:107)

Why did you create your enterprise? What happened was that I became a widow, I was alone. Because of that I studied, thinking about my future, my daughters, what are they going to have? Besides I thought that they were women and they were going to need this, right? It was more of a way out for me.

(Rosaluz Piura, 104:104)

Dissatisfaction with the family income. This circumstance is not necessarily associated with deprivations, but rather with the perception that the current income is not enough to cover the needs of the woman and her family. Even if it is enough to cover the basic expenses of the household, the family income is not enough to generate savings, to develop economically, to give better opportunities to her children, to have money for entertainment, and to have a better quality of life for the woman and her family. This dissatisfaction is a voluntary wish to have more than one has, and not a need for basic sustenance. It can be expressed as: 'We can live, but we want more income to increase our quality of life'. Four cases of women who chose to become entrepreneurs because of dissatisfaction with their family income were found, such as the cases of Miriam Médicis and Francisca Arequipa:

What happens is that you want certain things, certain comforts. And you can't. Or you want to improve something but can't. I mean, you have to limit yourself. That's it. That's what drove me to work more hours, to stay longer. I mean, I wanted to have better things. I didn't want to be with the same things.

(Miriam Médicis 100:100)

Here in Peru, if you don't make up your own source of work, what do you live with? You have to think 'what can I do', if my husband goes to work and gets a minimum wage, and if I go out, the same. And while we go out to work, our children are abandoned, that's what I've never liked, for the parents to abandon their children. That's what I say: Peruvians have to be creative, create their own enterprises, even if it is, I don't know, painting stones, making hair scrunchies.

(Francisca Arequipa 103:103)

The results show that women entrepreneurs have experienced the following work circumstances with regards to their decision to become entrepreneurs (Table 37 [Table 11.4]):

Difficulties in finding a job. This circumstance refers to the fact that the woman does not find a job because of lack of opportunities in the work market for her skills, because of her age or for not having enough education to allow her to find a dependent job. It can be expressed as: 'I have always been an entrepreneur, I did not find work opportunities for me, and entrepreneurship was my option'. Two women were found with in this situation, Teresa San Borja and Margarita Lima:

> Because there was a moment I was looking for a job and I said: 'now, what do I do? I can't find a job'. But in a moment I said 'I have to start and I have to do it myself'.
>
> (Teresa San Borja 235:236)

> When you're over 30 or 35, you don't get a job anymore, even though I have friends that give me a job in a restaurant, for example. But that takes a lot of effort.
>
> (Margarita Lima 24:25)

Lack of prospects for professional growth. This circumstance refers to the woman having few possibilities of a promotion in her dependent job; she perceives that getting promoted or having a better work position is too hard. She considers she cannot continue improving her work position and this generates frustration. This can be stated as: 'I have a job, but I can't go any further'. This lack of prospects for professional growth can happen because of lack of opportunities or owing to non-explicit discrimination. Sometimes there is an invisible barrier that makes promotion impossible in her job position. It is not about them not having enough income to cover their needs or desires, but about not feeling the satisfaction of their own professional and work prospects in their dependent job. The results show four cases of women who chose entrepreneurship when faced with a lack of prospects for professional growth in an independent job. Such are the cases of Gabriela Molina, Liliana Minera, Bety Lima and Cecilia Moy:

> Because we faced the need of creating an enterprise since our career went upwards. Because it went upwards, it would reach a point when we wouldn't be able to achieve many management positions … or higher. Then we said: 'What else will there be in the future for us'. Being young and very young managers. Then we said 'there must be something we can do.' Something of our own. Something if this ends one day. A '*stable*' job, shall we say, because there are no stable jobs nowadays. What's left for us? Then we decided to start an enterprise.
>
> (Gabriela Molina 229:229)

(Continued)

(Continued)

> As I told you, I got kind of tired of that job. I knew I couldn't get any higher, and I knew I could do more … I stood it there for a couple of years. I was already annoyed with it. I have always been a warrior, a fighter, so it was a little because of my character.
>
> (Liliana Minera 97:97)

> *Did you feel stagnated in your job?* Yes, it was too little for me. I wanted more, to be something more. That was my goal.
>
> (Bety Lima 95:95)

Frustration with the job owing to economic reasons. This circumstance refers to the situation where the job the woman has, or those she can get, do not pay her what she considers she deserves or what she thinks she needs to feel satisfied, and therefore she considers herself inadequately paid. It can be stated as: 'I have a job, but I don't like it because I earn too little'.

It is important to bear in mind that, in Peru, dependent jobs for people with a low educational level mean really low wages, in some cases even close to the survival level. Entrepreneurship turns out to be an alternative for people who consider themselves capable, but that have not had access to the education needed to have a good position in a dependent job. Three women from the study chose to become entrepreneurs because they felt inadequately paid in dependent jobs: Enit Moyobamba, Jesusa Rímac and Francisca Arequipa:

> Because when I worked with him, I realized I was the potential of his salon, I realized people came in looking for me, the motivation I had to do the job … Then I looked at my income, because back then I earned 500 soles a week, although he only gave me 30 per cent, I did my calculations and with what I produced I could pay rent, helpers. I paid attention to my income, and that encouraged me a lot to take off and progress.
>
> (Enit Moyobamba 202:203)

> *Did you ever consider you were being inadequately paid?* Yes. When I started working, I got paid too little and it wasn't enough even for bus fare. So that's also why I wanted to learn one day and be able to move forward.
>
> (Jesusa Rímac 224:225)

Dissatisfied with the male culture in her work environment. This happens when women are dissatisfied with the male culture in their work environment; that is, when a dependent job does not offer them the same conditions and opportunities as it does for men, for example, when a woman perceives that she is being offered less opportunities for promotion than men are, or less pay for the same level of responsibility.

The results show that women do not perceive this situation or that they evaluate it in a different way than the literature shows (Carter and Cannon, 1992). None of them declared feeling that a male culture in the work environment had prevented them from reaching a work position. On the contrary, they consider that the male culture is another challenge to prove their work capability. When referring to situations where they had to face a male culture, women answer by pointing out how they were able to overcome those male culture barriers. This does not mean that male culture has not prevented them from reaching a better dependent job position, but shows women do not perceive it that way. The cases of Jesusa Rímac and Ruth Apurímac show this perception:

> *Do you feel you were discriminated against for being a woman in any of your former jobs?* Well, I don't think so, because I've always been seen as a fighter, a strong woman. And they never discriminated me.
>
> (Jesusa Rímac 220:222)
>
> *Do you think that the male attitude of thinking 'women can't' was a factor for you to start your enterprise?* Yes, I am more encouraged to do better, to show them I can.
>
> (Ruth Apurímac 204:206)

Logical continuation of professional growth. This circumstance refers to women with a wide experience in a dependent job, who consider entrepreneurship as the logical continuation of their professional growth. It can be stated as: 'I have worked all my life, now is the moment to have something of my own'. Such is the case of Gabriela Molina, who considered it was the time to start her own enterprise, because she had had enough experience as self-employed.

The results show that women entrepreneurs have experienced these family circumstances with regards to their decision of becoming entrepreneurs (Table 37 [Table 11.4]).

Role of the woman in the family. This circumstance appears when the entrepreneurial activity is deeply connected to the role of mother and her function in the family. Results show that the purpose of the women is: (a) to involve their children in their enterprises so that they learn their operation; (b) to enable their children to have access to a better educational level than the women attained, so they can apply that knowledge to improve the management of the enterprise; (c) to generate their own source of work for their growing children; (d) to give their children the capacity to develop themselves and face life's ups and downs; and (e) to give economic security to their family, the kind of safety they yearn for. Six women showed a relationship between their entrepreneurial activity and their role inside the family; Silvia Lima and Liliana Piccolo among them:

(Continued)

(Continued)

How did you come to own the enterprise? Well, the first one was when my Dad was sick, as I told you before. The fear that something might happen to him and that all this would go bankrupt and we would end up with nothing. I am a person who has come a long way, and I know what it is like to be at the bottom. And that encouraged me too. I want for my family ... to have more in the future ... things I don't have. And the experience I am getting, if God allows it someday, can open a bigger enterprise, my own enterprise. Leave this enterprise to my siblings and for Loan Soul Graphic to be known internationally. That's what I wish for.

(Silvia Lima 190:190)

Which were your objectives and your vision when you started your enterprise? When I saw that the business was growing, I opened two more pizza parlors. I opened a third one. I gave two to one of my sons, and one to the other. They left them to go to the United Stated and Rome. They left them, sold them. But I started three.

(Liliana Piccolo 221:222)

Family succession. This circumstance refers to the situation where women choose entrepreneurship through family succession. The woman entrepreneur enters the entrepreneurial environment following a family line of succession, in which the father/mother/tutor gives her the possibility of working and managing the family enterprise to continue with the enterprise in the future. Family succession can be voluntary, or because of an opportunity or need.

Voluntary family succession is when the woman entrepreneur has the initiative, because she wants to work in the family enterprise. The family enterprise turns out to be the natural way of entering the world of work. In the cases in which the woman entrepreneur becomes such as a product of family succession, previous work experience is not necessarily related to the line of business of the enterprise, which holds more weight than the family background.

The succession by opportunity happens when a relative offers the woman the chance to become part of the enterprise, as is the case of Lorena Boston. Family succession by need happens because of an obligation; a family circumstance forces the woman to enter the family enterprise. In the cases in which the woman does not enter into the enterprise voluntarily, she is usually not prepared for it. Two women who chose entrepreneurship by family succession because of need (such as Silvia Lima) and voluntarily (such as Lorena Boston), were found:

How did you come to own the enterprise? Because of family succession. Because of the need itself. Because of the worry that something could happen to my dad. This way the enterprise would be in my hands and my family would be protected.

(Silvia Lima 149:150)

Did you have any special reason to become an entrepreneur? Let's say life took me there and I did it. That is, it's not something I thought about too much, really. As I told you, since I was little it was: 'Lorena will take control of the enterprise', 'Lorena has the qualities' ... so I didn't think much about it, really. I got in somehow, and I really like it. I like what I do.

(Lorena Boston 107:107)

The results show that women entrepreneurs have experienced these personal circumstances with regards to their decision to become entrepreneurs (Table 37 [Table 11.4]):

Presence of an entrepreneurial model. This circumstance refers to the existence of an entrepreneur who plays the role of reference for the woman, a source of knowledge and a model for the women to emulate or use as previous experience before creating their enterprises. The entrepreneurial model is the example of entrepreneurial activity for the woman, gives her courage in her decision to become an entrepreneur and allows her access to the knowledge needed to develop her enterprise.

Results show that 22 out of the 24 informants had an entrepreneur as reference (Table 39 [Table 11.6]). Ruth Apurímac had her mother and her first boss as entrepreneurial models, both in the bakery business; her mother always 'encouraged me', 'I did the best for her', and her boss allowed her to learn the bakery business. Silvia Lima had her father as an entrepreneurial example; Enit Moyobamba had her boss as an entrepreneurial model; Gabriela Molina did not have a direct entrepreneurial example, but she took her references from Peruvian entrepreneurs who succeeded and are socially acknowledged because of that; Carmela Arequipa had a relative as reference; and Monica Surco and Teresa San Borja had their parents as entrepreneur references. Table 39 [Table 11.6] shows the pattern observed in the analysed cases.

Dad was never interested in the business, but Mom was; she raised her four children in such a way that she sent us to different places to learn more about bakery, since there was no university were we lived.

(Ruth Apurímac 51:51)

(Continued)

(Continued)

I worked three years with my teacher, one with him and the other two with his brother. He had hairdresser salons in Miraflores, Surquillo, Rímac. *What did you learn there?* I learnt a lot: to run a hairdresser salon, to deal with clients, to have good sense, to manage some situations.

(Enit Moyobamba 85:89)

I have always admired people who start from scratch and succeed, as in the case of the Wong family. The case of the Añaños family, from Kola Real. I have always liked to investigate, to read about these successful experiences of diverse entrepreneurs in the country, and there are a lot. And through my political life I could lead in some way. Not through a position, but through research. The approach I have had with different kinds of persons, communities, population. I have benefitted from the successful experiences of lots of people.

(Gabriela Molina 269:269)

When I was in school, in Arequipa, I helped my godfather, who sold clothing. He sold clothing for a living, had a stall in the centre of Arequipa.

(Carmela Arequipa 27:27)

My parents were already merchants, both of them. My dad had his mechanics and lubricants shop. And my mom sold vegetables. And finally, the pig farm. Her last job.

(Monica Surco 98:98)

Which experience or training prepared you to be an entrepreneur? Working with my dad.

(Teresa San Borja 87:88)

Table 11.6 Women entrepreneurs reference models

Reference model	Cases	Frequency
Parents	Rosa, Silvia, Ruth, Enit, Jesusa, Mónica, Teresa, Lorena	8
Former boss	Liliana1, Rosaluz, Ruth, Enit, Jesusa	5
Relative	Francisca, Carmela, Edna, Lidia, Vilma, Margarita, Marcelina	7
Non-related entrepreneurs	Gabriela, Miriam, Bety	1
Husband	Rosaluz, Gloria	2
Uncle	Liliana2	1
No models, but has teachers	Doris	1
With no evident model	Cecilia	1
Total		24

Note: A case can be classified more than once N=24

The existence of people who motivate and support entrepreneurship. This circumstance is found when the woman entrepreneur has people close to her (parents/tutors/relatives/partner/husband) who encourage her towards entrepreneurship. They can be: parents who encourage the personal and professional development of their children through better educational levels and access to opportunities; models who represent examples of work and achievement; partners who promote entrepreneurship, etc.

The results show that this circumstance is found in most women entrepreneurs; the women describe having people close to them who encouraged them towards entrepreneurship, a father figure or a partner who promoted the creation of the enterprise. This type of support has a very important component of emotional support; that is, the presence of some relative, friend or acquaintance that motivated her and encouraged her to create the enterprise. In many cases, this role is assumed by the parents or husband/partner of the woman entrepreneur.

Table 40 [Table 11.7] shows the people who have supported the entrepreneurial activity of the informants. Gabriela Molina had her father and mother, who instilled in her the wish for improvement and the love of study through their example; her father was born outside of Lima, migrated to the capital to become a professional and became a doctor. In the case of Ruth Apurímac, her mother made it possible for her children to have a higher educational level, she motivated the family wellness. Ruth Apurímac had her mother as a permanent motivator, she told her 'you were not born to receive orders, but to give them'; 'she always encouraged me'. Enit Moyobamba had the support of her husband; Teresa San Borja had the support of her father; and Gloria Lima had her father's example.

What do you think of the people who still work for others? I think it all depends on the situation they're in; their willpower and the support they have has a lot to do with that. I had the support of my husband.

(Enit Moyobamba 90:91)

What kind of support do you receive from your relatives or contacts that allowed you to develop better your enterprise? From my dad, yes. Hey daddy look, I'm going to do such and such a thing, what do you think? Let's say, if someone gives me advice on entrepreneurial matters, it is my Dad. Or if I'm going to make this expense or not. Open the nursery, purchase. For example, that was a whole big deal. My dad is the one who gives me advice and approves.

(Teresa San Borja 189:190)

I've had a father who has been my example of perseverance and struggle. He has been a big example for me … maybe I got the tenacity from him.

(Continued)

(Continued)

I never heard him complaining or wailing. Rather, one of his mottos was that, when you asked him 'how are you', he answered: 'I'm fighting, because life is a constant fight, and I will stop fighting the day I die'.

(Gloria Lima 39:39)

Table 11.7 People who support women entrepreneurs' enterprises

People	Cases	Frequency
Parents	Silvia, Ruth, Teresa, Gloria, Margarita, Edna, Cecilia, Bety, Rosa, Liliana1, Rosaluz, Lorena	12
Husband	Lidia, Francisca, Doris, Enit, Jesusa, Gabriela, Mónica, Gloria, Carmela, Liliana1, Rosaluz	11
Siblings	Ruth, Rosa, Miriam	3
Son	Marcelina	1
No support	Liliana2, Vilma	2

Note: A case can be classified more than once N=24

Personal dissatisfaction. Women entrepreneurs can start an enterprise 'to have something important to do', when their economic needs are covered and they are looking for a source of personal satisfaction rather than economic income. This circumstance was found in two women, as is the case of Liliana Piccolo:

Why did you decide to establish your restaurant? No: I started the business because I had to do something. When I finished my job, I didn't work for a year, playing day and night. And I told myself: 'This can't go on, let's do something'.

(Liliana Piccolo 182:182)

Specific opportunity. A specific opportunity occurs when the woman faces an opportunity to start an enterprise and decides to take on the challenge, oriented towards the entrepreneurial activity. This is the case of Monica Surco, who worked at a hairdresser salon that stopped operating; she had the option of having the place transferred to her and become the owner of the enterprise she worked for. It is also the case of Vilma Mundo, who was a street vendor but was asked to leave by the municipal government; this motivated her to open a formal business in a shop instead of continuing with street sales. If such specific circumstances had not happened, these women would probably not have chosen the entrepreneurial activity.

Need for a flexible schedule. The need for an schedule that allows women to combine their responsibilities at work with those at home, and having a better quality of life, as dependent jobs tend to be very demanding and limiting for the role of mother and for family life, is a circumstance mentioned in the literature (Carter and Cannon, 1992; Orhan and Scott, 2001). However, the results show that this circumstance does not have an important effect in women choosing entrepreneurship. The need for a flexible schedule would be associated with the desire to spend more time with the children or doing the housework, but women entrepreneurs, instead of having more time for family activities, face longer work days than those of a dependent job.

Motive of achievement. The results show that women entrepreneurs have expressed motives of: *achievement, autonomy, affiliation* and *power* through their discourse. With regards to *achievement*, women entrepreneurs have stated that entrepreneurship is a source of personal satisfaction. The motive of *achievement* is expressed in the women through: (a) their impulse to 'reach a dream'; (b) their high capacity to work to achieve their goals; (c) the passion they feel for their entrepreneurial activity; (d) their active success-searching attitude; (e) their personal, professional and economic improvement attitude; (f) their capacity to take on challenges; (g) their 'do things better than others' attitude; (h) their high motivation to learn; and (i) their motivation to reach economic success.

Drive to reach a dream. Some women express 'reaching a dream' they have always had as a motive, regardless of the economic resources they have or their educational level. It would be possible to consider that women entrepreneurs with a low educational and economic level become entrepreneurs exclusively out of economic need. However, these cases show that the lack of education and economic resources is not decisive in defining entrepreneurship by an economic need. In this group of women, 'reaching a dream' is mentioned more than just the economic issue. Facing a lack of economic resources, these women could have sought a dependent job, but they considered it absurd to look for a job if they had the capacity needed to start their own enterprise. Five women expressed that 'reaching a dream' motivated them towards becoming entrepreneurs, Gabriela Molina and Miriam Médicis among them:

Did you always want to be an entrepreneur? I always had this feeling that I could do something by myself. *A need for achievement?* Maybe for a new challenge.

(Gabriela Molina 276:279)

What made me ... what happens is that I've always wanted to have my own thing since I was very young, something mine, it's as if you have something inside you that tells you 'Well, you can't work for others, you have to have your own thing, work for yourself'. They say that, at the beginning, it is like a staircase, like steps: at first you work for others,

(Continued)

(Continued)

then you work for yourself, and then you give others work. I think those
are the stairs you climb on your way to success, as they say. Well, I
never stopped to think I had to give employment to others, but now I am
thankful for that.

(Miriam Médicis, 96:96)

Work and personal effort capacity. The results prove that women
entrepreneurs show high dedication to their work activities, they find personal satisfaction in these activities, and have a high capacity to work.
Twenty women specifically showed a great passion towards work; the
cases of Gabriela Molina, Carmela Arequipa, Enit Moyobamba and Ruth
Apurímac show these motives clearly:

You always see me loaded with work. Of course I have defects, like
every other human being. And I think one of my big defects is that I am
a workaholic.

(Gabriela Molina 143:143)

No, I've always wanted to work; I even told him if I could go with him
to collect fares on the bus, but no, it has always been my idea to want to
work, or to have something of my own, right?

(Carmela Arequipa 93:93)

Yes, not easy at all, how many things I've sacrificed … While I was pregnant
I had to wake up at 6 am, I had to clean the floor of the business because
I had to open the next day. 'The place can't be closed for one day', I said,
that's why when I changed the flooring; I did it on a Sunday, the whole day.

(Enit Moyobamba 289:291)

At the time it was all effort and effort, I didn't sleep for more than two
hours, I almost didn't sleep, for me it was all work and more work, I went
to sleep at 1 am and got up at 3.

(Ruth Apurímac 98:100)

No, I'd die without work. I like working.

(Ruth Apurímac 122:124)

Passionate about what they do. Women entrepreneurs are passionate for
their enterprises, their job is not only a source of income, it is a source of
satisfaction. Ten women evidenced this motive, including Gabriela Molina
and Carmela Arequipa:

Work for me is really a joy. And that's what I try to teach my children.
That they have to do whatever they undertake with love and passion.

Really, that passion to do all things you undertake in life. Do things with love and a lot of patience.

(Gabriela Molina 137:137)

I've always liked to cook, always. Then I started working with that lady because of my sister, who recommended me, and she and my brother-in-law told me they liked my cooking.

(Carmela Arequipa 123:123)

Active search for success. Women entrepreneurs show an active attitude towards the search for success in their activities. Twenty-three women showed this attitude motivated by success. Enit Moyobamba, Ruth Apurímac, Liliana Piccolo, Vilma Mundo and Monica Surco show how they searched for success:

For example, I was a businesswoman since I was seven. *How come?* I sold everything because, as I told you, my parents were farmers. I sold bananas, oranges, cilantro … there was everything for me to sell. *Did you parents ask you to do it?* No, they never forced me to, it's just that I saw so many things go bad, like the bananas, and I said 'Why don't I sell them?'

(Enit Moyobamba 1 42:48)

I wanted something of my own, my house, and a car because I didn't have one … I got my apartment with Mi Banco.

(Enit Moyobamba 240:241)

Of course, I was active and he wasn't. He was happy on a minimum wage. He complained, he said 'You like working too much; you should give us some space'.

(Ruth Apurímac 88:88)

I started as a secretary, but my boss realized very soon that he could send me to the campsites, to his supplying partner. He sent me to the World Bank. I fixed things up for him. That's how I ended up having my own secretary. I worked myself up to the management.

(Liliana Piccolo 231:231)

I have always been very stubborn when I want something, but within limits. I have always been very … I've never been close-minded, I've always been open-minded. I set myself a goal and I have to make it there.

(Vilma Mundo 120:120)

Regardless of the bad experiences I had. I took over the place on 7 October, 2002. And the whole salon was burgled on 25 February, 2003.

(Continued)

(Continued)

I ended up with no capital. I did barbecues, raffles, services for my clients, and I started over again ... I was robbed again on 11 January, 2004. But like that, this time completely. No one is going to stop me, and I kept going. I called my suppliers. They refinanced my debt and gave me more credit on products and machinery. And that's how I started again.

(Monica Surco 54:54)

Permanent wish for self-improvement. Women entrepreneurs show a permanent wish for personal, professional and economic improvement, they are eager to learn everything they can and look to perfect themselves more and more. Seven women showed a permanent wish for improvement; Jesusa Rímac and Gabriela Molina clearly show their wish for improvement:

Why did you decide to create you enterprise? Yes, to be big. To be big and one day depend on what is mine. And I have really lived with some Arabs that were really, really rich. So I have really lived in a really luxurious house. I have eaten good food. I said: 'Why can't I live like this too?' I can too. I was young. That's what led me to create my enterprise.

(Jesusa Rímac 219:219)

Did you always want to be an entrepreneur? I always had this feeling that I could do something by myself... Maybe a new challenge.

(Gabriela Molina 276:279)

Capacity of undertaking challenges. Women show an attitude towards taking up challenges and grabbing opportunities. Sixteen women presented this motive, including Enit Moyobamba, Mónica Surco and Gloria Lima:

This lady asked me, because she saw me looking for a job every day, that's when she told me: 'My friend needs an stylist, it's an A1 salon in San Juan de Lurigancho', 'but it's a pity you're not a stylist', then I answered: 'of course I am an stylist', because I was desperate, I showed her my certificate of a basic course I took for a year, and then she decided to recommend me for the job, and gave me a letter to go to San Juan de Lurigancho.

(Enit Moyobamba 61:61)

No. It's just that the owner ... In this salon ... three owners came and went. I stayed with every owner that opened the hairdresser salon. I stayed .... Suddenly he said: 'I'm going to close the place'. I said 'ah, well then'. I was going to go back to work in an accountant's office with a friend. And one of the clients told me: 'Monica, you know how this works, why don't you take the chance?' And that's how it began. I started with two armchairs, two mirrors. There were days I didn't work at all.

(Monica Surco 44:44)

Well, I must have worked with him doing deliveries, sales to other people, I must have worked for four years, maybe three years ... and then I had the initiative of having my own space ... I always took it as a personal challenge, my own challenge.

(Gloria Lima 21:25)

Do things better than the rest. Women entrepreneurs show a desire to perfect themselves, a high level of commitment and perfection in their activities, and the wish to assume more responsibilities that those directly entrusted, which distinguishes them from other people. Eight women showed this motive, such as Enit Moyobamba, Gloria Lima and Ruth Apurímac:

Because when I worked with this gentleman, I realized I was the potential of his salon, I realized the people came looking for me, the motivation I had to do the job, people even mistook me for the owner in each salon I worked in, because of the will, the devotion I had for each job, because I was always checking and helping.

(Enit Moyobamba 202:202)

Look, I don't know if it is better, but it's just that when you do something, I think, you have to do it right, you must do it right.

(Gloria Lima 337:337)

I was interested in all the operation. From selling, handling cash to administering the workshop. Sometimes the cashier didn't come and I, without knowing much, handled the cash register and since the owner trusted me a lot, he gave me the cash register's key without any problem. I had earned his trust in those three years. I was like the owner's right hand. When I got bored, I closed my cash register and went to the workshop to see what the chefs were doing.

(Ruth Apurímac 125:127)

High motivation to learn. Women show a great motivation to learn new things, a curiosity that allows them to continue learning throughout their lives. Eight women expressed this motive, such as Jesusa Rímac, Teresa San Borja and Gloria Lima:

(Continued)

(Continued)

> *Did you have any experience in your youth that contributed to your decision of starting your own enterprise?* Yes, I worked in the house of very important people. People with a lot of money, who treat you bad sometimes because you're the housekeeper. And well, that's what encouraged me to learn someday and be someone. Maybe I couldn't study because I didn't have the chance. My mother was very young, I was very young, I was 8 years old. But I wanted to learn something. To get ahead.
>
> (Jesusa Rímac 246:247)

> Then I decided to start this business because of these reasons. One, because I had already worked in everything. I liked working. And I always wanted to work like this, with children. That was when I travelled to see how it works. I went to the United States. I was in Buenos Aires with someone who does this kind of things.
>
> (Teresa San Borja 195:196)

> Well, let me tell you that as I used to go to those organizations of events things, all that was training and everything, I went to courses, then they refreshed my memory.
>
> (Gloria Lima 638:639)

Achieving economic success. This circumstance refers to the fact that a dependent job does not allow some women to achieve economic success, while the possibilities for economic success with entrepreneurial activities are unlimited. Some women become entrepreneurs to 'be rich', as you 'will never be a millionaire' in a dependent job. Five women became entrepreneurs to achieve their own economic success, including the cases of Jesusa Rímac and Carmela Arequipa:

> *Why did you decide to create your enterprise?* Yes, to be big. To be big and one day depend on what is mine. And I have really lived with some Arabs that were really, really rich. So I have really lived in a really luxurious house. I have eaten good food. Why can't I live like this too? I can too. That's what led me to create my enterprise.
>
> (Jesusa Rímac 219:219)

> When I was with the father of my children, I said: 'When I have my own business I will buy my own clothes, my shoes', the things I need, right? Or buy things I needed at home. I am doing all that, little by little. Though there's still a lot to do, right? A long way to go.
>
> (Carmela Arequipa 543:543)

Motive of autonomy. The second motive the results show is that of *autonomy*. Autonomy is expressed in women through: (a) the need to 'be you own boss' and the fact that 'I don't like anyone giving me orders'; (b) autonomy with regards to the partner or family; (c) the need to control their own lives; (d) having something they can control and through which they can express themselves; and (e) autonomy in decision-making.

Seven women indicated the wish of 'being their own boss', such as Ruth Apurímac and Rosa Santa María:

> My mother always told me: 'My girl, you were not born to receive orders; you have been born to give them'. I always remember she said that ... I felt really good then, my Mom is right, I always had that in mind, when sometimes the owner made me work too much, from 15 to 16 hours, it was too much, and I only felt better with what Mom said, and I always kept it in my mind, and I always say it to my children too.
>
> (Ruth Apurímac 153:155)

> I didn't need anybody else to order me around, because our parents weren't ordered around either. Be ourselves, have our own things, being proud of what we had.
>
> (Rosa Santa María 112:112)

Autonomy is also expressed when entrepreneurial activity allows women to achieve economic independence with regards to their husbands/partners or family; when women change from being the passive half of the partnership and from being economically dependent on their partners or relatives to achieving their own value, this fills them with pride and satisfaction. The motive that encourages entrepreneurship is economic, but not out of economic need, but for autonomy. Four women expressed *autonomy*, Ruth Apurímac, Jesusa Rímac and Carmela Arequipa among them:

> I had to pay for it all myself, no one helped me. *And your parents?* I told my parents not to send me anything because I was working. I needed things, but I liked to do things by myself.
>
> (Ruth Apurímac 41:45)

> *Why did you decide to start your own enterprise?* To have my own time. My own money. It was nice.
>
> (Jesusa Rímac 260:262)

(Continued)

(Continued)

I've always wanted to work. I've always worked, that is, since I am here in Lima I have always wanted to have my own money, not depending from my partner or for anyone, even if I earn little. I have always liked to work.

(Carmela Arequipa 330:330)

Six women, such as Carmela Arequipa and Liliana Minera, expressed that their entrepreneurial activity allows them to control their own lives:

More than anything, to be independent. I was already tired of working as a slave for others, because when Christmas or Independence Day came, they gave me a 10 soles bonus.

(Carmela Arequipa 842:842)

What do you think about being independent What do I think? That it is really good, really. Being able to manage your times, even if you have to sacrifice more and all the responsibility is yours, because when you're an employee you get out at 5 and the problems stay in the business. But it is good. Especially when you have your own family. Being able to go to, when my children were little and acted at a school play, there are Moms that can't go; they are not allowed to go. Or when your son is sick and you stay with him and don't have to go to the office, then it's really good.

(Liliana Minera 105:105)

Seven women expressed their autonomy through the need of having something of their own, something they could control and through which they could express themselves, among them Gabriela Molina, Teresa San Borja and Monica Surco:

Then we used to say 'What else will there be in the future for us'. Being young and very young managers. Then we said 'there must be something we can do.' Something of our own. Something if this ends one day ...

(Gabriela Molina 229:229)

I always liked the business. I always wanted to generate something on my own, but I didn't know what. And then the salon opportunity presented itself.

(Monica Surco 270:270)

What motivated you to start your enterprise? Two things: One, I always wanted to have something of my own. And two, in the market, there wasn't what I wanted to do.

(Teresa San Borja 193:196)

Autonomy in entrepreneur women is also made evident in their independence in making decisions. These women do not need nor wait for their parents, husband or other figures of authority to approve their plans or decisions. Seven women presented this expression of their motive of autonomy, such as Ruth Apurímac and Carmela Arequipa:

I make the decisions, I tell Paco, 'Paco, I am doing this'.

(Ruth Apurímac 205:205)

The satisfaction of feeling that something is yours ... of course, it is yours, and if you want to earn a little more, you sacrifice a little more, or if you want to increase your capital, your sales, you do more, or put some, for example, if I want to put some dishes on the menu, I put them and do.

(Carmela Arequipa 845:846)

Motive of power. The third motive results show is that of *power.* Women expressed power through their desire for status, having an active leadership role in groups, and organizing and directing the activities of other people. The entrepreneurial activity for these women is a way of showing their own value to themselves and to others. Three women expressed the motive of *power* in their decision to choose entrepreneurship, Ruth Apurímac and Silvia Lima among them:

My Mom always comes here. When she knew I was working in a bakery, she was very happy, and she always told me: 'My girl, you were not born to receive orders, but to give them'. I always remember that she used to say that.

(Ruth Apurímac 53:53)

I always wanted a little power. And now I have it. And that also fills me with pride and satisfaction.

(Silvia Lima 241:242)

Motive of affiliation. The fourth motive the results show is that of *affiliation.* The motive is expressed through the entrepreneurial activity and is a social value, as it acts as a frame for a big part of the interactions established throughout life. Doris España expresses it as:

I think that, as I told you, showing what I am capable of doing. What made me do it? I mean, if my parents were both successful, if my relatives were successful, why couldn't I? I didn't want to be the ugly

(Continued)

(Continued)

duckling in the family. If I had my parents, who could do everything they wanted to, who could have all the money they had and could cover go all the way they did, why couldn't I? What do the other entrepreneurs have that I don't?

(Doris España 104:104)

Emerging Conceptual Framework: Why Do Women Become Entrepreneurs?

The results of the study and previous literature have given rise to the creation of the following conceptual framework to explain the diverse factors that have stimulated women to choose entrepreneurial activity (Figure 2 [Figure 11.1]). The conceptual framework considers two dimensions: (a) the phase of personal and work cycles when women choose entrepreneurship; and (b) the circumstances and motives that have stimulated women to become entrepreneurs. The circumstances and motives that have influenced the women's decision to choose entrepreneurship are not mutually exclusive; that is, the same person can be simultaneously influenced by several circumstances and motives.

Diverse studies in developed countries have explored the possible motivations of women entrepreneurs, but have not yet integrated them into a conceptual framework that integrally explains why women become entrepreneurs, bearing in mind their background and the factors that stimulated them to choose the entrepreneurial activity. Besides, the investigations that analyse the motivations of women entrepreneurs do not differentiate clearly the circumstances from the motives for choosing entrepreneurship, and present lists of isolated factors

The Life Cycle of Women Entrepreneurs

The results show that the women entrepreneurs' backgrounds are varied in terms of demography, education, family and work, and cannot be considered as a single category. The study shows that women entrepreneurs differ from one another in their demographic characteristics and in their educational, work and family backgrounds.

These results are not consistent with Hisrich and Brush (1984), who found that women entrepreneurs in the United States have similar family background, education, work experience, entrepreneurial characteristics, management skills and motivation; and that most women entrepreneurs are the first born of middle-class families in which the father was self-employed; half of them are married to men employed in professional or technical activities, and have two adolescent children on average; almost 70 per cent have basic education and many have university titles; their parents and husbands also have a good educational level; most of them do not have management knowledge, they have limited work experience, and when they do have it, it is in the area of services as teachers, middle level management employees or secretaries.

It is not enough to establish a unique profile of women entrepreneurs considering a single dimension, because it would be an inadequate simplification of their backgrounds. The profile of women entrepreneurs must be established considering the stage in their work and personal life cycles when they choose entrepreneurship. Carter and Cannon (1992) point out that the way in which women face the start of their entrepreneurial activity is controlled by the stage in their life cycle in which this happens, that is, their age and domestic relations. They indicate that the differentiation by life cycle is important because women start their enterprises at different stages of their lives and this affects the type of enterprise and the particular approach to ownership. Besides, Carter and Cannon (1992) point out that the previous work experience generates diverse motivations and aspirations with regards to enterprise ownership.

The results of the study show that women entrepreneurs can be grouped by their common experiences in the stages of their life cycle when they choose entrepreneurship. In order to categorize women into the phases of their life cycles, the following characteristics related to their background have been considered: (a) stage of life when they choose entrepreneurship (husband/partner children); and (b) stage of professional/work experience measured in the number of years of work experience previous to entrepreneurship. The age when they choose entrepreneurship has not been a determinant for the life cycle categorization, as this does not depend on the years, but on the experiences of each person.

The phases of their life cycle when women choose entrepreneurship that have arisen in the study are shown in Appendix M (Women entrepreneurs according to their life cycle).

Phase I: Young women. This phase is essentially defined by the lack of dependents and relatively scarce or non-relevant work experience. This group includes women who decide to become entrepreneurs in the first phase of their family life cycle, when they have no children, may or may not have a husband/ partner and have little work experience. Entrepreneurship for these women may be the product of a natural option (such as voluntary family succession or entrepreneurial spirit) or be due to the absence of other work alternatives.

Five women informants chose entrepreneurship in phase I of their lives. They were all single and with no children. One of the women did not have previous work experience, while the others did have some work experience in dependent activities. The case of Vilma Mundo is unusual, as she started working as a street vendor when she was a child. The informants in this phase chose entrepreneurship before they reached 27 years old.

(Continued)

(Continued)

Phase II: Growing women. This phase is essentially defined by the existence of dependents and intermediate work experience. This group considers women who choose entrepreneurship in the middle phase of their life cycle: They usually have economically and emotionally dependent small children, though they may not; some are married or have life partners, others are separated, or divorced or may have or not have a partner; they have regular work experience. These women have chosen entrepreneurship after having abandoned their dependent jobs or other independent activities.

Thirteen informant women chose entrepreneurship in phase II of their life. Three women had no children, while all the others had small or older dependent children. Their work experience is over seven years, except in the case of Doris, who had less work experience but had dependent children when she chose entrepreneurship. Informants in this group chose entrepreneurship between 26 and 38 years of age.

Phase III: Consolidated women. This phase essentially defines women who have advanced work experience, with or without dependents. This group includes women who have dependent young children or economically dependent children, even though some may have no children. In any case, they have work experience of over 20 years and decide to become entrepreneurs in the last stage of their work cycle, as the goal of their work development or the logical continuation of their professional development. These women choose entrepreneurship as a result of a lack of work opportunities, or are women who, eager to develop their own independent entrepreneurial activity, accumulate work experience as dependent employees and then leave a paid job in order to establish an enterprise as the goal of their professional path.

Six informant women chose entrepreneurship in phase III of their lives: they all had older dependent children and had more than 29 years of work experience. All are established women in terms of work experience. These informants chose entrepreneurship after they were 35 years of age.

Typology of Women Entrepreneurs

Results show the diverse patterns the women followed, according to their life cycle and the factors that stimulated them to become entrepreneurs. The conceptual framework presented makes is possible to understand the different profiles of women entrepreneurs, taking into consideration their background and factors that motivated them to become entrepreneurs.

The conceptual framework distinguishes between the circumstances referred to as *happenings* and *situations*. A *suceso* [happening] is defined as a 'cosa que sucede, especialmente cuando es de alguna importancia' (Real Academia de la Lengua, 2001) [something that happens, especially when it has some importance] and in the present study, refers to objective happenings that affect the woman's decision to become an entrepreneur, such as the death of the father in a family business, or the loss of a dependent job. A *situación* [situation] is defined as 'disposición de una cosa respecto del lugar que ocupa' (Real Academia de la Lengua, 2001) [disposition of something with respect to the place it holds] and refers to the factors that influence a woman's decision to become an entrepreneur, and that depend on the woman's own perception, such as her dissatisfaction with the family income or her lack of prospects for professional growth.

The circumstances referred to as *happenings* are: basic economic need, family succession by need, difficulty in finding a job and frustration with work because of economic reasons. The circumstances referred to as *situations* include: dissatisfaction with the family income, by opportunity or voluntary family succession, role of the woman in the family, lack of prospects for professional growth or as continuation of professional development, personal dissatisfaction or specific opportunity. The motives are present in all cases of women entrepreneurs, so they have not been used as criteria to differentiate the profiles.

The emerging conceptual framework reinforces the results, in that women cannot be considered as a homogeneous group with unique characteristics and that the profile of women entrepreneurs must be expressed through a typology that represents their different experiences. The matrix of case analysis is presented in Appendix N, showing the different existing combinations between the cycle of life and the factors that influence entrepreneurship. The summary of the matrix is shown on Table 42 [Table 11.8] and Figure 2 [Figure 11.1] shows the emerging conceptual framework. The analysis identified six profiles of women entrepreneurs that express the different paths through which women reach entrepreneurship. The profiles that came up from the study are:

Table 11.8 Matrix of cases categorized by life cycle stages

	Happening [a]	*Situation* [b]
Phase I	3 cases	2 cases
Phase II	5 cases	8 cases
Phase III	4 cases	2 cases

Notes:

a Basic economic need, family succession by need, difficulty to find a job, frustration for economic reasons.

b Dissatisfaction with family income, family succession, by opportunity or voluntary family succession, role of the woman in the family, lack of perspectives of professional growth, continuation of professional development, personal dissatisfaction or specific opportunity.

(Continued)

(Continued)

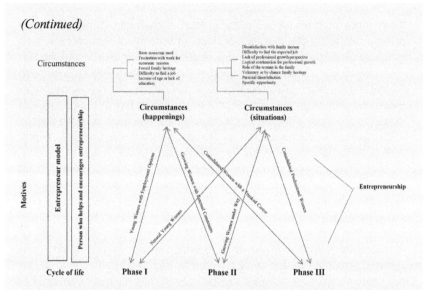

Figure 11.1 Emerging conceptual framework: why women become entrepreneurs

Young women with employment options. This group comprises those women that have chosen the entrepreneurial activity in the face of happenings that gave them no other choice than entrepreneurship and whose work choice resulted in an entrepreneurial activity. These are women who are in the first phase of their personal and work life cycle; they have no children or dependents, and have little work experience. The educational level of this group of women is usually only basic education, which limits their work options. These women choose entrepreneurship without any previous preparation, which is why they develop their own experience within the enterprise itself and are less prepared for entrepreneurial activity than women with other identified profiles.

The case identified in this group refers to forced family succession, which was what happened to Silvia Lima, who had to take up the family enterprise in view of her father's illness; and to Vilma Mundo and Marcelina Áncash, who chose entrepreneurship mainly to cover their basic economic needs. Vilma only had basic secondary education, and Marcelina only had basic primary education.

> I became an entrepreneur … by a circumstance, rather than an experience. Considering that my dad was alone in the enterprise. The moment came when he got sick and I was scared … if something happens to Dad, this will go bankrupt … The fear that something could happen to him and that everything could go bankrupt and we'd end up with nothing.
>
> (Silvia Lima 150:150)

Why did you open your enterprise? Need. Poverty and hunger were killing me at 6, 7 and 8 years old...I had to defeat hunger and poverty. That was my mission and my task. And I had to do it, and I did it with effort.

(Vilma Mundo 107:107)

The last job I had was that of street vendor. I sold cakes, chicha morada, jell-o ... My husband helped ... I sold chicha in the mornings and pudding, jell-o in the afternoons. Then we started the bakery, in partnership with his cousin ... we got a place in Comas. We've been there for 18 years.

(Marcelina Áncash 33:33)

Grown women with external constraints. This group comprises those women who have chosen the entrepreneurial activity in the face of happenings that gave them no other work alternative, because of some kind of external limitation. These women have chosen entrepreneurship in the second phase of their work and personal life cycle, after having some work experience. They usually have economically dependent small or older children, and may or may not have a husband/partner. The educational levels of this group of women are varied, but they usually have technical or higher education. These are women who have worked dependently and have acquired some work experience. They have chosen entrepreneurship mainly because of economic reasons: to cover their basic needs or because of the frustration in not getting sufficient pay in their dependent job.

The cases of Gloria Lima and Lidia Puno belong to this profile. They chose entrepreneurship mainly to cover their basic economic needs. Gloria Lima created her enterprise when faced with her partner's economic problems. Lidia Puno created her enterprise in view of her inability to continue her occasional activities in artisan fairs. Francisca Arequipa and Enit Moyobamba, who chose entrepreneurship because of their frustration at receiving minimum wages that did not offer them any economic security for their families or themselves, also belong to this group. They developed important work experience, sought opportunities and chose entrepreneurship after having worked for a salary. Edna Marsano also developed work experience and was forced to take over the enterprise her husband had created, owing to her partner's lack of responsibility to make the family enterprise work and to cover the family's economic needs.

Here in Peru, if you do not make up your own source of work, what do you live with? You have to think 'what can I do', if my husband goes to work and gets paid a minimum wage, and if I go out, the same thing happens. And while we go out to work, our children are abandoned, that's

(Continued)

(Continued)

what I've never liked, for the parents to abandon their children. That's what I say: Peruvians have to be creative, create his own enterprises, even if it is, I don't know, painting stones, making hair scrunchies.

(Francisca Arequipa 103:103)

Why didn't you stay working as an employee in the hairdresser salon? Because when I worked with this gentleman, I realized I was the potential of his salon, I realized the people came looking for me, the motivation I had to do the job, people even mistook me for the owner in each salon I worked in, because of the will, the devotion I had for each job, because I was always checking and helping.

(Enit Moyobamba 202:202)

Look, I had a debt of about 400,000 soles to pay, I had only saved 60,000 soles and I had to pay in six months, in about six months, which was the time they had given me to pay off all that debt ... and the shop caught fire. I've had to refinance, go to enterprises to talk for them to help me, or some approached me themselves and gave me bills of exchange for a year ... I put a lot of effort to go on forward. Because of that I took over the shop.

(Edna Marsano 120:120)

Consolidated women with unfinished undergraduate studies. This group comprises those women who have chosen the entrepreneurial activity when faced with happenings that gave them no other work alternative, and whose dependent activity has been cut short. These women have chosen entrepreneurship in the third phase of their personal and work life cycle, after accumulating considerable work experience. They may or may not have children, and if they do, these are already young adults. These women have been obliged to choose entrepreneurship as an answer to their frustration with economic factors. They may have not become entrepreneurs if had they had been satisfied with their dependent jobs. For them, entrepreneurship offers the option of covering their basic economic needs. Although these women had no preparation before entrepreneurship, they have work maturity, and reach entrepreneurship with vast work experience.

The cases of Jesusa Rímac, Carmela Arequipa, Rosaluz Piura and Margarita Lima, who chose entrepreneurship because of the frustration of receiving minimum wages that did not offer economic security for their families or themselves or cover basic economic needs, belong to this profile. They built up important work experience, sought opportunities and chose entrepreneurship after more than 20 years of working in a dependent job.

Yes, I worked in the house of very important people. With people with a lot of money who sometimes treat you bad because you're the housekeeper. And well, that was what motivated me to someday learn and be someone. Maybe I couldn't study because I didn't have the chance. My mother was very young, I was little, I was 8 years old. But I wanted to learn something. To get ahead.

(Jesusa Rímac 246:247)

Why did you decide to start you own enterprise? Above all to be independent. I had already gotten tired of working as a slave for others, because when Christmas or Independence Day came, they gave me a 10 soles bonus.

(Carmela Arequipa 842:842)

Why did you decide to start your own enterprise? What happened is that I ended up alone, I was a widow. I studied because of that, thinking about the future, in my daughters ... It was another way out for me ... you have to think, think about the future. You want to be stable. You can't go from one job to another forever. Besides, age is also an issue. More than anything, to have something on your own. Not working for someone else forever. You realize you can do it by yourself.

(Rosaluz Piura 104:104)

For example, once you're past the age, who takes you in? When you're over 30 or 35 years of age you don't get jobs anymore ... I like working as a teacher, but the salary is too low ... but you want to have something on your own.

(Margarita Lima 111:111)

Natural young women. This group is formed by those women who have chosen the entrepreneurial activity as a naturally desirable work alternative. These women can be considered as 'natives' of entrepreneurship. They are entrepreneurs from the first phase of their personal and work cycle, they have no children or dependents and have little to none work experience. Their educational level may be basic or superior, what is relevant is their natural preference towards the entrepreneurial activity. These women have chosen entrepreneurship as the natural way of practising their work activity; such is the case of Teresa San Borja and Rosa Santa María:

What made you decide to start your enterprise? Two things: One, I always wanted to have something of my own. And two, in the market, there wasn't what I wanted to do. So I had to create this job because I didn't see myself doing anything else.

(Teresa San Borja 193:196)

(Continued)

(Continued)

Why did we start our business? I think that was born in us. To be independent, not to depend from others. We saw that our parents worked independently. It wasn't anything new for us, it wasn't a thing from outer space, it was the natural thing to do, having a business.

(Rosa Santa Maria 104:104)

Grown women under way. This group is formed by those women who have chosen the entrepreneurial activity as a personal development option after having accumulated work experience as dependent workers. These women have 'migrated' from dependent activity to entrepreneurship as an alternative to professional development. They have taken the choice of entrepreneurship in the second phase of their personal and work life cycle, after having some work experience. They usually have economically and emotionally dependent small or older children, and may or may not have a partner.

They are women that have worked dependently and have accumulated some work experience, and have chosen entrepreneurship because of situations such as a voluntary family succession; lack of prospects for professional growth in dependent jobs; considering entrepreneurship as the logical continuation of their professional development; or because they are dissatisfied with the family income that, even though enough to cover their basic needs, does not allow them to satisfy their expectations for a better quality of life. These women have not experienced happenings external to them that have prevented them from choosing other work alternatives, but the situations they perceive depend on their own perspective. The educational level of these women is varied, but all of them have entered the entrepreneurial activity after having gained the necessary knowledge through their work experience.

The cases of Miriam Médicis, Gabriela Molina, Liliana Minera, Mónica Surco, Lorena Boston, Bety Lima, Doris España and Cecilia Moy belong to this profile. Miriam chose to start her own medical centre because she was dissatisfied with her independent activity as a dentist; Gabriela Molina developed her building enterprise parallel to her dependent work activity because she considered she did not have prospects of professional growth in her dependent activity, and left her job when the enterprise reached the size she expected. Liliana Minera decided to create her own enterprise to trade machinery replacement parts after she learnt about the business in another enterprise, and because she considered that she had reached the limit of her dependent professional career. Monica Surco considered herself capable of taking over the hairdresser salon where she had worked for several years when the main partners retired, and she took the opportunity to create her own enterprise. Lorena Boston faced the voluntary family succession in the enterprise created 56 years before by her father. Bety Lima was frustrated in her job as a teacher in the public sector and decided to create her own school for children with the experience obtained. Doris España decided to open her tourism enterprise after having analysed the market opportunities, and prepared herself by studying tourism before opening her own enterprise. Cecilia Moy decided to open her own enterprise dedicated to money exchange and financing after acquiring the necessary skills by working as a dependent employee in the bank industry.

What made me create my enterprise …. what happens is that, ever since I was little, I've always wanted to have something on my own, it's like you have something inside you that says: 'Well, you can't work for others, you have to have your own thing, work for yourself'.

(Miriam Médicis 96:96)

Why did you decide to create your own enterprise? No. It's just that the owner … In this salon…three owners came and went. I stayed with every owner that opened the hairdresser salon. I stayed …. Suddenly he said: 'I'm going to close the place'. I said 'ah, well then'. I was going to back to work in an accountant's office with a friend. And one of the clients told me: 'Monica, you know how this works, why don't you take the chance?' And that's how I began.

(Monica Surco 44:44)

Why did you decide to create your own enterprise? I wanted something of my own. Do my own thing. I didn't have any more there, that is, nowhere to grow. Because over me there was my boss, the owner of the enterprise, I couldn't be her owner, and I don't know, I decided to start my own enterprise.

(Liliana Minera 40:40)

Why did you decide to create your own enterprise? Because we faced the need of creating an enterprise; because our career went upwards. Because it went upwards, it would reach a point when we wouldn't be able to achieve many management positions … or higher ... Then we said 'there must be something we can do.' Something of our own. Something if this ends one day. A *'stable'* job, shall we say, because there are no stable jobs nowadays. What's left for us? Then we decided to start an enterprise.

(Gabriela Molina 229:229)

Why did you decide to create your own enterprise? Not really. Let's say that life got me there and I assumed that role. I mean, it's not something I thought too much about, really. As I told you, since I was little it was: 'Lorena will take the control of the enterprise', 'Lorena has qualities' … so I didn't think much about it, really. I got in somehow, and I really like it. I like what I do.

(Lorena Boston 107:107)

(Continued)

(Continued)

> *Why did you decide to create your own enterprise?* That encouraged me to have my own enterprise, because I did work a lot for the Government. I worked a lot for my community, but there was always that discrimination, because I liked to be outstanding in everything, and that hurt, I said: 'Why?' I give everything I have. And I earned very little. And there came a time, thanks to this person who told me: 'Why don't you open on your own, you can do it and you have the place and everything'.
>
> (Bety Lima 98:98)

> *Why did you decide to create your own enterprise?* Money. Basically money ... you could be an excellent worker and you could be just a genius, do a lot of positive things, and you didn't earn more for that. The other thing was that, at that moment and for many more years, you couldn't get promoted.
>
> (Cecilia Moy 39:39)

Consolidated professional women. This group is formed by those women who have chosen the entrepreneurial activity as the culmination of their work development, and after having gathered important work experience as dependent workers. These women have 'migrated' from dependent activities to entrepreneurship as the culmination of their work career. They have chosen entrepreneurship in the third phase of their personal and work life cycle. They may or may not have children, and if they do, they are young adults. They are women who have always worked for others and now want to work for themselves. They are women who have chosen entrepreneurship because of situations such as dissatisfaction with their current income or with their work as dependent workers; their decision is also related to the possibility of fulfilling their role within the family and generating work opportunities for their children and relatives. These women have not experienced happenings external to them that would have prevented them from choosing another work alternative, it is just that the situations they perceive depend on their own perspective. The educational profile of these women is varied, but they have all entered entrepreneurial activity after having acquired the necessary knowledge through their work experience, which is why they face entrepreneurship more prepared than women entrepreneurs from the rest of profiles, in work and personal terms.

The cases of Ruth Apurímac and Liliana Piccolo belong to this profile. Liliana decided to choose entrepreneurship after retiring from a dependent job that demanded too many working hours for her wage. Ruth Apurímac worked her whole life with the idea of generating her own enterprise. Her bakery represents the culmination of her work efforts.

My Mom got very happy when she knew I was working in a bakery. She always told me: 'My daughter, you haven't been born to receive orders, you were born to give them'. I always remember she said that ... I always bear it in mind, and I always repeat it to my children too.

(Ruth Apurímac 153:155)

How did you become the owner of a restaurant? When I was done with the enterprise. I said, Liliana, what do you like to do? I grabbed a piece of paper, and the first thing I wrote was, a building company, but I didn't have the money; second thing, sewing, because I like to sew, but I hadn't sewn a button in 14 years; cooking, I like cooking, cooking: OK. Cook what? I grabbed another piece of paper, chose the kind of restaurant that wouldn't tie me so much with too many different inputs. I choose a pizza parlour. The next day I was looking for a place. The first Restaurant was born.

(Liliana Piccolo 28:28)

Final part

This chapter ends without including a summary or conclusions. The conclusions are included in the final chapter and it is unusual to present a summary.

Reference

Avolio Alecchi, B. (2010). El Perfil de las Mujeres Empresarias en el Perú. [An Exploratory Study of the Profile of Women Entrepreneurs in Peru]. DBA thesis, Pontifical Catholic University of Peru.

12 Conclusions and recommendations

This chapter includes the study conclusions, implications and recommendations. It consists of the following sections:

a) Conclusions
b) Contributions
c) Limitations
d) Recommendations.

Conclusions

The conclusions are a very important section because they reflect the analysis and the responses to the research questions. The conclusions should never be confused with a study summary, nor should they repeat the data that has already been presented. They should focus on answering the research questions and achieving the purpose defined in the study.

The conclusions should be numbered and written coherently and accurately. They must reflect the whole analysis. To enable a better understanding, they can be arranged with subheadings so as to order the sequence when there are several conclusions.

The following example of the conclusions is taken from Avolio's dissertation (2010):

Conclusions

Using the qualitative paradigm, this dissertation has responded to the following research questions: What are the demographic characteristics and educational, work and family background of women entrepreneurs? What are the administrative/managerial skills of women entrepreneurs? What are the characteristics of women-owned companies? What are the factors that stimulated them to become women entrepreneurs? And what are the main obstacles to start and develop women-owned companies?

The conclusions of the study are about the following:

The Demographic Characteristics and Educational, Work and Family Background of Women Entrepreneurs

1   Results show that women entrepreneurs seem to have a varied demographic profile; they seem not to form a homogeneous group and this is why they cannot be treated as a sole category. It does not seem appropriate to create a sole profile for women entrepreneurs because it would be an improper simplification of their characteristics and needs. Support programmes for women entrepreneurial activity should start with a diagnosis acknowledging the diversity of their backgrounds.

2   Women entrepreneurs seem to show varied demographic, educational and work profiles which leads to the conclusion that age, civil status, place of birth, birth order, education level, kind of education, type and sector of working experience are not factors that seem to characterize women entrepreneurs. These characteristics seem related to the profile of women in general and not particularly related to female business activity.

3   Educational background found in women informants points to four conclusions. First, women entrepreneurs seem to show different educational backgrounds which shows that the level and type of education are not factors that seem to characterize them. If it is true that a low educational level may represent an obstacle to the development and growth of their enterprises, educational level and type do not seem to be related to their entrepreneurial spirit. Second, the type of educational experience prior to entrepreneurship does not seem to be a determining factor in the nature of women-owned enterprises; the sector of women enterprises does not seem to be determined by their previous educational background. Third, it is apparent that women entrepreneurs have parents and husbands/partners with diverse educational backgrounds. This shows that such backgrounds are not determining factors; the educational level of women entrepreneurs' direct relatives does not seem to be related to their entrepreneurial spirit. Fourth, the small relationship between women's educational experience and the nature of their enterprises indicates that the education system does not seem to influence the generation of women's entrepreneurial spirit and that the opportunities for entrepreneurial development do not seem to be mainly based on educational background.

4   The working background found in the women informants leads to several conclusions. First, women entrepreneurs seem to have working experience prior to the entrepreneurship of diverse types and in different sectors and these are not determinant factors for women entrepreneurs or related to their entrepreneurial spirit and their decision of

(Continued)

(Continued)

choosing to become entrepreneurs. Second, it seems that women entrepreneurs usually have some working experience; they are active in the working environment and reach entrepreneurship as a result of a process of searching for working opportunities and not by chance. Third, the decision to create an enterprise seems to be influenced by previous working experience or by a woman's personal interest. Although the type of educational experience prior to the entrepreneurship does not seem to be a dominant factor in the nature of the women-owned enterprise, results confirm that the type of working experience prior to the entrepreneurship does seem to be in relation to the nature of the women-owned enterprises. This is especially true of women with experience as a dependent employee, in which case women create an enterprise 'doing what they can do'. In the case of women with no experience as a dependent employee, enterprises seem to be related to personal interests or developed household skills, in such a way that women create an enterprise 'doing what they like to do'. The only case in which previous working experience does not seem to be related to the current enterprise is when the enterprise has been taken up by family succession and working experience is not a relevant factor in the entrepreneurship. Fourth, results identify six profiles of women entrepreneurs according to the working circumstances prior to entrepreneurship: (a) women voluntarily leaving their employments to start a new business; (b) women voluntarily leaving their independent activities (professionals or self-employment) to create an enterprise; (c) women voluntarily leaving their employment to work full-time in an enterprise they created in parallel to their activity as dependent employees; (d) women voluntarily leaving their employment and choosing entrepreneurship on their own accord or because of the lack of other alternatives; (e) women leaving their employment for family or personal reasons, with no evident reason to create an enterprise, for whom entrepreneurship is a way to reinsert themselves into the working world; and (f) women that decide to become entrepreneurs in view of a specific opportunity.

5   The family background of women entrepreneurs points to some conclusions. First, the educational level of their parents and husbands/partners seem not to be factors that characterize women entrepreneurs and seem not to be related to their entrepreneurial spirit. However, results indicate that the parents' working activity seem to be a factor with some influence on their decision to become entrepreneurs, as usually women entrepreneurs come from families whose parents have been related to entrepreneurship, independent working activities or self-employment. Second, it seems that women trend to employ family members in their enterprises. This indicates that for women entrepreneurs, their enterprise

is another expression of their role as woman within the family and constitutes yet another means to assume their role as mother, daughter or partner. This is evident when the woman: (a) employs family members in her enterprise; (b) when husbands/partners that used to have dependent activities when women decided to become entrepreneurs become their business partners or employees of women entrepreneurs when their enterprises become successful; (c) wants her children to get actively involved in the enterprise; (d) tries to provide her children with a higher educational level than hers, so that they may use this knowledge to improve the enterprise management, to make them grow and to continue with family succession; (e) creates job positions for the family through her enterprise; (f) tries to offer the family economic stability through her enterprise. Third, it seems that women tend to choose to become entrepreneurs when their children are already older but still dependent, while is it less frequently the case of women opting for entrepreneurship when their children are small and dependent. This can be explained by the fact that women are mainly devoted to taking care of the children and have less time to start an entrepreneurial project. Fourth, although there is a clear feminization in working activities, traditional roles related to the house or child care seem to be mainly the woman's responsibility, which represents a disadvantage to compete in the entrepreneurial activity owing to the diversity of roles that they must play simultaneously. It seems that women face particular challenges related to their gender, in which they must be able to manage the roles of economic generation, house care and mother/wife/partner/daughter at the same time. Although women stated that they have the support of close relatives or domestic help to collaborate with taking care of the children and house chores, which is an important advantage in playing such roles, one of the main challenges that women entrepreneurs seem to face is trying to balance their family and entrepreneurial roles, as their entrepreneurial project leaves them little time for their children or personal affairs. This can generate tensions or conflicts regarding the administration of their priorities and time. However, the support from husbands/partners is evident, when applicable, in the development of the women's entrepreneurial activity by either economic or emotional support. Fifth, women express that their enterprises are part of their lives and that their entrepreneurial roles are not different from their family. Some women organize their enterprises around their relatives, establishing a priority in their family relationships. Other women do this the other way around: they organize their family relations around their enterprises in other words, they give priority to their business and family demands become a problem if they challenge their entrepreneurial role. For these women, the enterprise is

(Continued)

(Continued)

not an obstacle to their family life but the other way around: husbands/ partners may obstruct their entrepreneurial objectives and they will only stay together provided they do not become obstacles to their entrepreneurial projects.

The Factors that Stimulated them to Become Entrepreneurs

1   The driving factors for women to become entrepreneurs are a complex system of circumstances and motives that interact among them. In no case does there seem to be a sole circumstance or sole motive impelling women to become entrepreneurs.

2   The factors that stimulated women to become entrepreneurs can be classified as: (a) motives; and (b) economic, work, family and personal circumstances. In other words, events or situations that appeared in a certain context drove such women to become entrepreneurs. The motives have an origin intrinsic to women while circumstances are extrinsic to women and may impact entrepreneurship in a positive or negative way. These circumstances may be an objective event (such as the death of the father in a family enterprise or the loss of dependent employment) or situations impacting entrepreneurship according to the perception women have (such as the dissatisfaction with family income or lack of professional growth prospects).

3   The economic circumstances that affect the decision of becoming an entrepreneur are: economic need or dissatisfaction with family income. Working circumstances are: difficulty in finding employment owing to a lack of opportunities in the work market because of having no skills, old age, no education; lack of professional growth prospects; job frustration for economic reasons; or considering that entrepreneurship is the logical continuation of professional growth. Family circumstances are: when entrepreneurship is the means to comply with their family role; from a voluntary family succession, from opportunities or necessity. Personal circumstances are: an entrepreneurial model used as reference for women; relatives that promote and support entrepreneurship; personal dissatisfaction; or a specific opportunity.

4   There are two factors that seem to have an important influence on women entrepreneurs' decisions to become entrepreneurs and that have not been previously considered in the literature: (a) the existence of close people fostering, promoting and supporting their entrepreneurship or a paternal model or a partner that promoted the creation of an enterprise; and (b) the existence of an entrepreneurial model that works as a reference for women. In the first case, these are people close to the

women who encourage them towards entrepreneurship, help them in their professional and personal development, allow them the access to opportunities and provide them with models that are examples of work and achievement. This kind of support has an important component of emotional backing; that is, the presence of a relative, a friend or someone they know that fosters and encourages her to create the enterprise. In many cases, this role is played by the parents or husband/partner of women entrepreneurs. An entrepreneurial model, in turn, plays a role as referent for women; they constitute a source of knowledge about the entrepreneurial activity and an example to be followed or used by women as experience before creating their own enterprises. The entrepreneur is an example of entrepreneurial activity for the woman. It provides her with courage to become an entrepreneur and allows her to obtain the necessary knowledge to develop the entrepreneurial activity.

5 In spite of the predominance of the male culture in Latin American countries, women do not seem to notice as factors that have an influence on the entrepreneurship, frustration for a male culture in the working environment or the need of a flexible schedule to attend family responsibilities. These gender-related factors do not seem to have an important influence in women entrepreneurs even though they are frequently mentioned in the literature.

6 Women have expressed that *achievement* and *autonomy* are the motives that seem to have most influence in their entrepreneurship, while a small proportion have mentioned the motives *power* and *affiliation*. Informant women entrepreneurs have expressed in their discourse a high intrinsic motivation; in other words, they declare they feel compelled to develop their enterprises driven by a desire for achievement or that they find an intrinsic reward in their enterprises. Benefits sought by these women in their enterprises are not exclusively economic benefits: they seem interested in the success of their enterprise far beyond economic earnings. Therefore, faced with the possibility of giving up their job and living from their profits, they express that they prefer to continue working.

The Transversal Case Analysis

1 Women in Peru seem to be more motivated by 'pull' factors to entrepreneurship than by circumstances that 'push' them to choose the entrepreneurial activity. It could be assumed that economic conditions in Peru caused women to become entrepreneurs because of economic needs and that women entrepreneurs with a low education or economic

(Continued)

(Continued)

level become entrepreneurs exclusively because of economic needs. This study concludes that the lack of education and economic resources may be decisive in defining entrepreneurship but that the expressions of *achievement* and *autonomy* are factors that seem to be more frequent than economic circumstances in promoting entrepreneurial activity. Women with low education levels and the need to generate economic resources may have applied for a dependent job; however, they point out that it seemed absurd to apply for a dependent job if they had the skills needed to start their own enterprises. In this sense, it is debatable whether the decision of becoming an entrepreneur arises by obligation or by chance, not even in the case of economic need, but it is a choice over others and involves an inclination towards it. Economic need by itself, may lead to self-employment but not necessarily to entrepreneurial activity. Self-employment can be a way to survive in view of lack of education and economic resources, but the entrepreneurial activity involves an inclination by the woman towards the search of opportunities and the resources needed to carry out their projects.

2   Circumstances affecting entrepreneurship, as well as the obstacles women entrepreneurs face, seem to show differences according to their demographic, educational and family background. Older women entrepreneurs seem to be more influenced by economic circumstances than by work or personal factors in their decision of choosing to become entrepreneurs. In younger women, work circumstances (such as the difficulty in finding a job, the lack of professional growth prospects or working frustration for economic reasons) seem to be more frequent.

3   The group of women with a lower level of education seem to be more influenced by economic circumstances such as basic economic needs, insufficient family income or because of feeling frustrated owing to the fact that their work environment can only provide them with less income than they expect, in their decision of choosing entrepreneurship. The group of women with a higher educational level seems to be more influenced by work circumstances such as frustration for a lack of professional development prospects or because they consider that entrepreneurial activity is the logical continuation of their professional development.

4   The group of women with higher family responsibilities (dependent children) seem to be more influenced in their decision of choosing to become entrepreneurs for economic and family circumstances, which reinforces the evidence that, for women, the enterprise is part of their role within the family and a way to fulfil such a role by generating economic safety for their children and relatives.

5   By analysing the relationship between obstacles mentioned by women and their backgrounds, it is concluded that the lack of training to manage enterprises is an obstacle women face regardless of their education level; and that the difficulty of conciliating entrepreneurial and family responsibilities seems to be related to the number of children, the age of the children and the level of responsibility of women at home.

The Profile of Women Entrepreneurs

It seems that women entrepreneurs cannot be considered a homogeneous group with unique characteristics and that their profile must be expressed through a typology that represents their different experiences. Establishing a unique profile of women entrepreneurs considering a sole dimension seems to be an inadequate simplification of their backgrounds. The study proposes a conceptual framework that explains the profile of women entrepreneurs from the stage of the work and personal life cycle in which they opt for entrepreneurship (as women start their enterprises at different moments in their life and this affects the type of business and their particular approach to the enterprise ownership) and the factors that stimulated them to become entrepreneurs. Results have identified six profiles of women entrepreneurs that express different routes by which women achieve entrepreneurship, called: Young Women with Employment Options, Growing Women with External Constraints, Consolidated Women with a Trunked Career, Natural Young Women, Growing Women under Way, and Consolidated Professional Women.

Contributions

The contributions of the research refer to the study's input. The contributions are usually divided into two major groups: Theoretical contributions and practical contributions. The first refers to the study's contribution to existing knowledge and theory. The practical contributions refer to the study's contribution to social sciences practice.

Depending on the nature and purpose of the study, there may be both types of contributions or only one of them. Just as for the conclusions, the writing style should be concise and clear, and to the point.

Theoretical contributions

The following example of theoretical contributions is taken from Avolio's dissertation (2010):

Contributions

Theoretical Contributions

This research has contributed to entrepreneurship knowledge as an area for research in five aspects. First, the study has developed Orhan and Scott (2001) model to find empirical verification for the elements proposed. Second, it contributes with a clear definition of the *entrepreneur* concept and makes a difference with the concept of *self-employment*, which can constitute the basis of the concept for future researches. Third, it contributes the proposal of a conceptual framework to explain why women become entrepreneurs, integrating several circumstances and several motives that influence women in their decision and the relationship of these with their backgrounds. The conceptual framework identifies different circumstances and diverse motives related to entrepreneurial activity of women that the literature has not covered before. Fourth, the research develops the profile of women entrepreneurs and identifies six groups of women that represent the different routes that women take when opting for entrepreneurship, taking into account the factors that influence their decision of becoming entrepreneurs and the stage of their life cycle in which they take such a decision. Fifth, results provide information to develop a measurement instrument based on different dimensions of the profile of women entrepreneurs. Sixth, owing to the explorative nature of the research, results allow a hypothesis to be formulated for the development of different investigations in the area of women's entrepreneurship.

Furthermore, the originality and the value of the studies are found in the fact that it adds more evidence to current literature with respect to the characteristics, backgrounds, motives and obstacles women entrepreneurs have to face, in a context that has not been studied before. One interesting aspect of the context studied is that it represents the country with the highest Total Entrepreneurial Activity rate.

Practical contributions

The following example of practical contributions is taken from Avolio's dissertation (2010):

Practical Contributions

This research provides knowledge about the entrepreneurial activity of women in Peru, by identifying determined patterns in their demographic, educational, work and family backgrounds, their skills, factors that influence their decision to become entrepreneurs and the obstacles that they face. Results provide important knowledge of their entrepreneurial activity, identify the circumstances and motives impacting their entrepreneurship and present a typology of different profiles in women.

This knowledge will make it possible to develop policies to promote the creation of enterprises by women and to design specific support programs according to the specific profile of women entrepreneurs to stimulate their capacities adequately, decreasing their obstacles and increasing the chances for the success of their entrepreneurial efforts.

Study limitations

Even though the study limitations are presented in the introduction (Chapter 1), they are usually repeated in this section to clarify the limitations of the research conclusions.

The following study limitations example is taken from Avolio's dissertation (2010):

Study Limitations

This investigation has several limitations, which may be considered as the basis to improve future research.

First, it is not possible to generalize the results statistically for the population of women entrepreneurs; future research may expand the results of this study under a quantitative approach. Second, the study is focused in Metropolitan Lima; therefore the results are only valid for this geographical area. Third, the study only considers the formal sector of women entrepreneurs in spite of the importance of the informal sector in the country's economy. Fourth, the study is focused on enterprises with two or more years of formal operation, which may show a bias towards successful enterprises. Fifth, the study excludes self-employment, which may be considered as entrepreneurial activity by some researchers. Sixth, the study only analyses women entrepreneurs without comparing them with men entrepreneurs. Future research may consider both men entrepreneurs, and women entrepreneurs to establish if there are substantial differences between genders.

Seventh, the study samples women entrepreneurs who, at least, have met the minimum definition of a going business concern and who have overcome the initial stage of the entrepreneurial development (2 years of operations). In this sense, the conclusions of the study regarding the profile of women entrepreneurs (demographic, educational, work and family background, administrative/managerial skills and nature of their enterprises) and the factors that have motivated the women to choose entrepreneurship are focused on businesses that may be considered successful. The businesses that failed in their initial stage were not taken into account in the sample

(Continued)

(Continued)

and may be the subject of further study to analyse the existing profile and motives of women entrepreneurs, contrasting their profile with those businesses of women enterprises that failed.

With regards to the obstacles that women face, the study explores the obstacles for women entrepreneurs in the development of their enterprises. It may be considered that if better policies are to be recommended, there should be an analysis of the women who wanted to be entrepreneurs but for some reason were prevented from succeeding, given that whatever obstacles they faced, the women in this sample have obviously overcome them. However, the study is focused on the obstacles that women entrepreneurs currently face in continuing to develop their business, because the two years they are in operation does not prevent these businesses from failing in the future. In this regard, it is important to analyse these obstacles in order to increase the life expectancy of the businesses in the future and to enable further growth. Future studies on female entrepreneurship could compare women who failed in their entrepreneurial attempt with women who were successful, in order to improve the initial attempts for the development of a business enterprise.

Recommendations

The recommendations are the final part of the research. The researcher is expected to make recommendations in two areas: practical recommendations oriented to study field practice, and recommendations for future researches based on literature gaps and issues that arose throughout the research process.

Just as the contributions, the language used in the recommendations should be clear and accurate. It is advisable to number the recommendations and present the practical recommendations separately from the recommendations oriented to further research.

Practical recommendations

The following practical recommendations example is taken from Avolio's dissertation (2010):

Recommendations

Practical Recommendations

Based on the results of the study, the following practical recommendations are presented, aimed at public policies and support programmes related to women entrepreneurship.

First: It is recommended to establish national statistics on entrepreneurial activity in general, and in particular those collecting information on gender aspects, as currently they are scarce and contradictory, a fact that limits knowledge on entrepreneurial activity in general, and especially on women entrepreneurial activity.

Second: It is recommended to establish a clear definition of the concept of *entrepreneurial activity*, clarifying the difference from *self-employment*. Self-employment may mean a way of living in view of economic need, but entrepreneurship implies an inclination towards the search for opportunities and resources for the development of the entrepreneurial project. Many studies and policies make no difference between self-employment and entrepreneurial activity, which produces confusion in the analysis.

Third: Although women constitute an important and growing proportion of entrepreneurial activity in Peru, support programmes have been developed without a deep knowledge about the reality of women entrepreneurs. Women entrepreneurs seem not to constitute a homogeneous group and cannot be considered as a sole category. Women entrepreneurs apparently constitute a complex group and have diverse backgrounds, skills, circumstances and motives, and obstacles. Support programmes and policies should start with a deep knowledge about women and be developed specifically for each type of women entrepreneur.

Fourth: The weak relation between educational backgrounds and the nature of women-owned enterprises shows that the local educational system has no influence in encouraging entrepreneurship. The reason may be that the current educational system does not encourage entrepreneurship. It is thus recommended that the educational system be studied with the goal of improving its promotion of entrepreneurial activity. If an educational system established the foundations for the promotion of entrepreneurial activity, it could have an impact on the development of entrepreneurial activity.

Fifth: The existence of an entrepreneurial model, as well as the support from people close to the entrepreneur, has appeared in the study as an important pattern for entrepreneurial development. Therefore, women may take advantage of a formal 'mentoring entrepreneurs' programme, in which women entrepreneurs offer their *mentoring* to women that are only just starting their entrepreneurial activity. The purpose of this programme would be that the new entrepreneurs: (a) obtain more confidence about their entrepreneurial orientation (b) learn about the management of an enterprise in a practical way; (c) obtain knowledge and guidance in the most deficient areas; and (d) develop more confidence in their own entrepreneurial capabilities.

Sixth: Women entrepreneurs with work experience before becoming entrepreneurs are better prepared for the entrepreneurial activity than those who had no experience. It is recommended that women entrepreneurs have

(Continued)

(Continued)

work experience before starting an enterprise, because this may increase their confidence for decision-making, as well as giving them more information about the way an enterprise works.

Seventh: From the study results and the experience from programmes developed in other countries, the programmes oriented at stimulating women entrepreneurship should consider the following areas: (a) advisory and consultancy; (b) training in business management; (c) financing; (d) access to information; and (e) a network of contacts. The purpose of advisory and consultancy guidance is to stimulate women that wish to become entrepreneurs, by studying their skills, offering them support to start their enterprises, to plan and develop their enterprises; dealing with the specific problems faced by women entrepreneurs; and give them a clear picture of the degree of dedication necessary to develop an enterprise and the capacity to balance their family and entrepreneurial responsibilities. Training aims at improving women's skills in business management, by training them in specific topics and developing in them the capacity of raising the necessary human capital to promote their enterprises. Through training women should be able to acknowledge their own weaknesses and know how to hire the people they need to handle these areas. Access to financing should be facilitated, the system of collaterals required should be simplified and, most important, the cost of credits for women entrepreneurs should be reduced. Access to information about markets, new products, business development and management will enable women to expand opportunities for their businesses. Although the need for a network of contacts has not been mentioned as an obstacle for the development of the enterprises by women entrepreneurs, it is present in the literature and in the experience of other countries. A network of contacts enables women to interchange experiences with entrepreneurs and professional organizations and increase their opportunities to create enterprises, and is a useful source of inspiration. The network of contacts and the access to information expose women to a wider business environment and allow them access to opportunities to increase their own potential as entrepreneurs.

This last recommendation may not be deduced only from the study, and simply ratifies the findings from previous studies regarding the needs of women entrepreneurs. The originality of this study, however, is its recommendation that the programmes oriented to stimulating women entrepreneurship cannot be the same for all women; they must recognize that women do not seem to be a homogeneous group (as women start their enterprises at different moments in their lives and for different reasons, and this affects the type of business and their particular approach to business ownership). For example, a network of contacts is more relevant for Natural Young Women than for Consolidated Professional Women, who are more likely to have an adequate network of contacts as a result of their work experiences.

Recommendations for future research

The following example of recommendations for future research is taken from Avolio's dissertation (2010):

Recommendations for Future Research

Based on the results and limitations of the study, ten areas of future research about entrepreneurship are proposed:

First: Expand the results of this study to a quantitative phase to generalize the results to the population of women entrepreneurs, including not only entrepreneurial activity in Lima, but throughout Peru.

Second: Expand the results of this study to a quantitative phase developed in several countries in Latin America, to obtain comparative information about the profile of women entrepreneurs.

Third: Validate the emerging conceptual framework under a quantitative methodology, studying the relations between identified circumstances and motives and the decision to become entrepreneurs.

Fourth: Compare women's with men's entrepreneurial activity, to find out if women's and men's backgrounds, motives and obstacles are different.

Fifth: Analyse the relationship between the identified profiles of women entrepreneurs and the success of entrepreneurial activity, in order to identify those profiles with the highest probability of success in their enterprises. That is, do natural entrepreneurs have more chances to succeed than the ones that became entrepreneurs by need, do women entrepreneurs with experience in dependent jobs have more chances to succeed that those with no previous work experience?

Sixth: Analyse the relationship between the factors that stimulated entrepreneurship and success in entrepreneurial activity; that is, do women who become entrepreneurs for a basic economic need have fewer chances to succeed than entrepreneurs stimulated by dissatisfaction with their family income?

Seventh: Entrepreneurs, regardless of their gender, should inspire others to follow their dreams and should be able to attract and keep valuable collaborators. In this sense, does gender represent an obstacle to attract valuable collaborators? What is the perception of leadership in business management? How many talented professionals would be willing to have a woman as their boss?

Eighth: Expand knowledge about women entrepreneurial activity in Latin America, studying individual, organizational, process and environmental aspects. In the first group, the proposal is to carry out studies on personality, motivation and on executive women that leave their dependent jobs to become entrepreneurs. With regard to organizational aspects,

(Continued)

(Continued)

the proposal is to study the organizational characteristics of women-owned enterprises, the reason for success or failure in women-owned enterprises, and growth and development patterns of women-owned enterprises. The aspects related to process are aimed at studying administrative practices (management styles, strategies) in women-owned enterprises: Which are administrative practices of women entrepreneurs? What administrative practices are related to successful businesses? Concerning the environment, the proposal is to carry out studies regarding the specific barriers women entrepreneurs have to face, the perceptions of women as entrepreneurs, and the conflicts in the enterprise/family/person roles.

Ninth: Study the capacity of the educational system to promote entrepreneurship: Are entrepreneurs born? Is it possible to 'create entrepreneurs'? Do business schools, universities and schools have the capacity to 'create entrepreneurs'? Is entrepreneurial 'incubation' only destined for people who were born to become entrepreneurs? Is it possible to anticipate and identify who may become an entrepreneur?

Tenth: Compare the enterprises of women who failed in their entrepreneurial attempt with the enterprises of women that were successful, in order to identify the obstacles that they faced to start and develop their businesses.

Reference

Avolio Alecchi, B. (2010). El Perfil de las Mujeres Empresarias en el Perú. [An Exploratory Study of the Profile of Women Entrepreneurs in Peru]. DBA thesis, Pontifical Catholic University of Peru.

Index

Note: **bold** page numbers indicate figures; *italics* indicate tables.

For Product Safety Concerns and Information please contact our EU
representative GPSR@taylorandfrancis.com
Taylor & Francis Verlag GmbH, Kaufingerstraße 24, 80331 München, Germany

www.ingramcontent.com/pod-product-compliance
Ingram Content Group UK Ltd.
Pitfield, Milton Keynes, MK11 3LW, UK
UKHW021031180425
457613UK00021B/1125